CHINA

KOREA

JAPAN

PACIFIC OCEAN

Ryukyu Is.

Bonin Is.

Taiwan

VIET-
NAM

CAMBODIA

PHILIPPINES

Mariana Is.

Wake

Guam

Marshall Is.

MALAYSIA

Caroline Is.

SINGAPORE

NAURU

PAPUA NEW GUINEA

Ocean

INDONESIA

Solomon Is.

Christmas

Vanuatu

Fiji Is.

New
Caledonia

AUSTRALIA

Norfolk

NEW
ZEALAND

THIS IS Papua New Guinea

Papua New Guinea

PUBLISHED BY THE PAPUA NEW GUINEA GOVERNMENT OFFICE OF INFORMATION

Published by the Papua New Guinea Government. Office of Information
© Papua New Guinea Government

ISBN 0 7247 0650X

July, 1980.

Printed in Hong Kong
by South China Printing Co.

THE NATIONAL EMBLEM

The National Emblem features a widespread Bird of Paradise, *Genus Paradisaea*, perched on a *Kundu,* a drum used for ceremonial purposes. Behind the drum is a spear.

The emblem is representative of all parts of Papua New Guinea since the three symbols appearing on it are well known over a wide area of the country. The emblem design was prepared in 1971 by a group of design artists from the Office of Information.

The Bird of Paradise is depicted in its different natural colors. It has a yellow head, grey-blue bill, black neck, green breast with yellow band, and light brown abdomen. The wings and long tail feathers are reddish brown while the display plumes are deep red.

The *Kundu* and spear are black with white highlights and ornamentations.

Use of the National Flag and the National Emblem is restricted to official government use as laid out in the National Identity Ordinance of 1973.

THE NATIONAL FLAG

The Papua New Guinea National Flag, formally adopted in 1971, is rectangular in the proportion of four to three. It is divided diagonally from the top of the hoist to the bottom of the fly. On the upper part appears a yellow Bird of Paradise on a red ground. On the lower part are five white stars, representing the Southern Cross, on a black ground. Black, red and yellow are traditional colors in Papua New Guinea.

The flag design was based on one made by Susan Karike, a 15-year old student from Yule Island in the Central Province. Susan's design was chosen from among many others submitted in a nation-wide flag design competition.

The Bird of Paradise plays an important part in the social and cultural activities of many groups in Papua New Guinea and its plumes are often used as ceremonial decoration. On the flag, it is shown soaring above the Southern Cross, with display plumes trailing, symbolizing Papua New Guinea's emergence into nationhood.

The Southern Cross is a constellation notable in the night skies of Papua New Guinea and other countries of the southern hemisphere. It appears on the flag to signify Papua New Guinea's historical relationship with Australia and friendship with other nations of the South Pacific.

Contents

Contents continued . . .

Introduction

On 16 September 1975 Papua New Guinea eagerly accepted its greatest challenge, to rule itself and take its place in the international community of independent nations.

Independence came in a cascade of exploding fireworks, the high point of a week of official celebrations, signifying the joy of the spirit unleashed, the start of a new and proud era.

The way in which these precious moments of destiny came about are almost as important as the actual event itself. The occasion had dignity. The colonial power was not brushed aside with raw nationalistic power as so often happens in the developing world. Independence was negotiated honorably and the birth of our nation was endorsed and witnessed by many nations.

The guiding principles by which we negotiated Self-Government and Independence have stood us in good stead in the years since 1975.

The challenge, met enthusiastically, has had its rewards. Our early years as a nation have seen the germination of the seeds of a just and democratic society. The ideals espoused in the Constitution have been upheld. The processes of parliamentary government have strengthened and national elections have been held.

A most important step in shaping our future has been the decentralisation of administration through the establishment of provincial governments.

Papua New Guinea glories in the diversity of its land and its peoples. We have great mountains and highland valleys, mighty rivers, vast marshes and swamplands, extensive coastal plains with majestic forests, and our legendary islands scatter in profusion about the tropical seas.

Even more, we are proud of the diversity and cultural richness of our different societies. It is not illogical to entrust to each major group the care and development of its area. Indeed, it should be seen as an acknowledgement of our common interest and mutual trust.

These first years of independence have coincided with continuing change and dislocation in the world, in politics, economics and trade.

So far Papua New Guinea has been largely sheltered from these forces. But we are not so cut off that we are not affected.

Our future is a continuing challenge and we intend to pursue with vigorous determination the policies and programmes that have served us so well in our early years.

The best opportunity for our people lies in the land. It has always been the basis of our lives and will remain so. The methods may change, new crops may be introduced, but the pattern of village families farming their land for subsistence and a saleable surplus is still a realistic and attractive dream.

Our affinity with the land is centuries old. The vast majority of our people still live in rural communities and for the well being of our nation this emphasis on rural development must be maintained.

We see no justification or benefit in sprawling urban development, quite the contrary, and Government policies will continue to be directed toward expanding our economic base in primary industries.

We believe we are fortunate that the many ills of the Western world have not been felt on a wide scale in our country. Inflation does not erode our wealth as quickly as it accumulates, industrialisation has not polluted our air, rivers and oceans. We have room to live and breathe peacefully.

Most important we have the opportunity to learn from the mistakes of others.

In this and other respects we believe we are unique.

This is Papua New Guinea . . .

Sir TORE LOKOLOKO G.C.M.G., O.B.E., K.St.J.
Governor-General of the
Independent State of Papua New Guinea

1

The land and the people:

The Land and the People

When the first astronaut set foot on the moon he made an historic statement about a small step for man but a giant step for mankind.

Although the beautiful, but sometimes hostile landscape of Papua New Guinea can not be remotely compared to a moonscape there are certain parallels between that first moon-walker's words and the situation that confronted the nation when it was born in 1975.

After a relatively short period of colonial administration, (most other third world countries were colonised for centuries) Papua New Guinea decided to plunge into the maelstrom of world affairs as a new and independent nation. . .

. . .A giant step indeed for a people relatively inexperienced in international affairs. Despite this inexperience the nation's fifth anniversary will be joyfully celebrated in 1980 and already our traditional trait of consultation and negotiation has been noted in international conferences as well as being instrumental in settling disputes at home.

Papua New Guinea is populated by a race of people speaking hundreds of languages, living in small coastal villages and on high mountain ridges. They have always lived with feet firmly planted on the ground and an awareness of the environment. The land and the spirits of ancestors dictated the pattern of life entirely.

Traditionally the people lived isolated lives. This was partly due to the difficult terrain but most probably because life was not easy. Each group jealously guarded what it had won from the land and sea from the incursions of neighbours.

Nevertheless, a certain amount of communication took place in that not so distant past. Marriages were made between tribes and trade went on which allowed close neighbours to live at peace with each other for most of the time.

Like the moon Papua New Guinea has always been there. If the reader were to pick up a history book he could be excused for thinking that 'New Guinea' was 'discovered' in the 16th century by one of a number of Portuguese or Spanish sea captains.

Of course this is not true. The land and the people have always been here. It is only the name, Papua New Guinea, that was given to us by those bygone seafearers.

Even that has changed over the years. Illpas dos Papuas (land of frizzy-haired people), Isla del oro (Island of gold), Nuvo Guinea, British Papua and a thousand other introduced names for the rivers, mountains, villages and later the towns and cities.

They may all change again but the land and the people will remain.

Physical features

Location

Lying between longitudes 141 and 160 East, and latitudes 1 and 12 South, Papua New Guinea forms the eastern half of the island of New Guinea, the world's second largest island. The western half, formerly Dutch New Guinea, comprises the Indonesian province of Irian Jaya. To the South is Australia, to the East the Solomon Islands, and to the North the Pacific Ocean.

Papua New Guinea formerly comprised the Australian Territory of Papua and the United Nations Trust Territory of New Guinea. It has a land area of 462 840 square kilometres, including the large islands of New Britain, New Ireland and Bougainville, and some 600 small islands and archipelagos. These islands represent the eastern end of the great arc of mountains which extend through the Himalayas and Malaysia into the Pacific and include some of the world's most rugged country.

The Land

The mainland and the larger islands are notable for their impressive mountain ranges. Several mountains exceed 4 000 metres, the highest being Mt. Wilhelm which stands 4 706 metres above sea level.

The main island is dominated by a central mountain chain or cordillera which extends throughout the whole length of the island. It is broken in many places by broad upland valleys and plains where primary products like coffee and tea are grown.

The mountains are the source of fast flowing rivers which descend to the coastal plains to join some of the world's largest swamp systems. Two of the country's largest rivers, the Sepik and the Fly, are navigable to small boats for about 800 kilometres.

A line of active volcanoes extends along the north coast of the mainland through the Island of New Britain. They form part of the Pacific 'Ring of Fire', an area of volcanic activity and earthquakes encircling the Pacific Ocean.

There are also volcanoes and hot springs in the south eastern part of the country and some of the other islands.

Rainfall

Rainfall figures vary dramatically in different regions of the country due to wind and altitude influences. Two places separated by only a short distance on the ground can have greatly different rainfall levels. A typical example occurs in the Markham Valley in the Morobe Province where annual rainfall at Erap is 1 270 mm compared with a mean of 4 617 mm at Lae, about 80 kilometres to the south east.

Port Moresby is comparatively dry with an average rainfall of 1 200 mm a year, and has strongly marked wet and dry seasons. During the wet season, precipitation is mainly a result

Morning mists rise from a highland valley after the night's rain.

Climate

Being in the tropics, and surrounded by warm seas over which its prevailing winds blow, Papua New Guinea has a generally hot and humid climate. However, conditions vary greatly from one area to another. This is because of the effect of the mountainous topography (high ridges and steep valleys) on the two major prevailing air streams, the south-east trade winds and the north-west monsoon.

of thunderstorm activity caused by moisture laden air being forced up over the inland ranges by the north-west monsoonal winds. In contrast, the southeasterly winds of the dry season run parallel to the coast and the Owen Stanley ranges behind Port Moresby, so little rain occurs at this time.

At the other extreme, most of the North Solomons Province receives rain all the year round. This province comprises mostly mountainous islands which are exposed to both

As the afternoon rains close in a woman staggers home from her garden under a heavy load.

prevailing air streams. The mountains lift the moist air and cool it, producing rain throughout almost all the year. Consequently, Boku on the west coast of Bougainville receives 6 350 mm of rain annually. Similarly, areas along the coast of New Britain and inland of the Gulf of Papua regularly record over 9 000 mm a year.

Temperatures

Temperatures in the lowlands and coastal areas are uniformly high, while in the highland region, days are mild to warm and nights are cool throughout the year. In the higher ranges frosts are common and snow occasionally falls on the highest peaks.

Mean temperatures are similar throughout the year with a daily average range of 9 degrees Celcius on the coasts and lowlands, and about 12 degrees Celcius in the highlands and mountains. Lowland temperatures reach a little over 30 degrees in the afternoon and fall to 22 degrees overnight. Goroka in the Highlands registers 25 degrees and 14 degrees for similar times of a day.

Slightly lower temperatures from May to October in the Papua and highland regions occur as a result of winter conditions in the southern hemisphere.

Extreme temperatures recorded for Port Moresby are 36 and 14 degrees, for Lae, 39 and 18 degrees, and for Mt. Hagen, 31 and 2 degrees.

Papua New Guinea is probably one of the cloudiest places in the world averaging from half to three quarters cloud cover throughout the year. Of the sunshine recording stations, Port Moresby does best with an average of 7 hours daily sunshine.

Relative humidity is uniformly high, about 75-90 per cent in the lowlands, decreasing to about 65-80 per cent in the Highlands.

Many highland valleys are carpeted with swamplands. Some have been drained and put to agricultural use.

Dendrobium malbrowni

Dendrobium antennatum

Dendrobium nindii

Flora and fauna

In terms of vegetation, Papua New Guinea is classified as part of the Indonesia-Malaysia region, though much of it is similar to that of Northern Australia.

Over 75 per cent of the land is covered with rich tropical rain forest. Plants and trees grow rapidly and luxuriantly because of heavy rainfall and high temperatures. Many trees grow to a height of 46 metres and more, their branches forming a canopy providing a rich environment for animals.

Many of the large trees have big buttresses and their branches support the growth of ferns, vines and parasitic plants. Different kinds of palms and canes are also common in the forest.

Swampy Forests

In the lowland areas, particularly associated with the high river systems, there are wide areas of swampy forests. The river banks provide a rich environment for the growth of vast stands of sago palm, a staple food in such areas, pit pit and wild sugar cane which grows to a height of 7 metres.

In flooded areas and around open lakes, many species of weeds, water lilies and water ferns grow in abundance.

On the coast, at the mouth of large rivers, mangrove trees grow up to a height of 30 metres. Nipa palm stands serve as a breeding ground for prawns and fish.

The dry areas around Port Moresby and western Papua are covered by savannah grass-land plains. Some trees, mostly Eucalyptus, occasionally grow among the kangaroo grass. These savannah woodlands are regarded as part of drier vegetation of northern Australia.

At altitudes above 1000 metres the lowland rain forest is replaced by a two-layered forest called the 'lower montane' type. Here, hoop and klinkii pines, two of the country's most valuable timbers, become dominant.

Oak trees become more and more common as the altitude increases.

Montane Forests

Between 2 000 and 3 350 metres altitude grow the montane forests where beech stands, conifer trees and mossy vegetation are common. At higher altitudes most of the trees are generally crooked and stunted in growth.

The alpine forest, above 3 350 metres, consists of tussock grasses, tree ferns and shrubs. This vegetation is very similar to the forest cover of New Zealand and Tasmania in Australia.

In some highland valleys and lowland areas, there are man-made grasslands. These have developed as a result of the frequent use of fire for clearing garden sites and for hunting. They consist of tall, coarse kunai grass, and shorter kangaroo grass, and have a potential for cattle raising and reforestation.

Animal Life

Papua New Guinea's animal life is as diverse as its landscape and vegetation. Its high mountains and wide lowland areas provide favourable environments for many kinds of animals, birds and insects.

The animals of Papua New Guinea are classified with those of Australia. Until 8 000 years ago the island of New Guinea was joined to the Australian mainland across what is now the Torres Strait and the Arafura Sea, and isolated from mainland Asia. Thus Australia and New Guinea have many animals in common.

Gowra Pidgeon

Mammals

Mammals are animals that feed their young on milk. Papua New Guinea has representatives of the three types of mammals — the monotremes, marsupials and placental mammals.

The monotremes, or mammals that lay eggs, are represented by 2 types of echidna. One is the short-snouted echidna which lives in the lowland savannah of the Papuan region. The other is the long-snouted echidna, which is found only in the highlands and is one of Papua New Guinea's National Animals.

National Animals are those animals in Papua New Guinea protected by law to prevent overhunting and to retain their traditional use. They may be hunted and used in traditional ways but may neither be sold nor hunted by modern methods. Aside from the long-snouted echidna, the National Animals include the New Guinea eagle, all the Birds of Paradise, goura pigeons, seven birdwing butterflies, and some kinds of egrets.

Placental mammals are represented in Papua New Guinea by only a few animals such as the dugong or seacow which is another national animal. The dugong is a shy animal that lives in shallow coastal waters and feeds on seagrasses. Because of overhunting, there are only a few of these left in the Indo-Pacific area.

Water barriers and distance from mainland Asia have prevented most orders of placental mammals from reaching Papua New Guinea. Due to this lack of competition, there has remained a large group of mammals called marsupials.

Marsupials are mammals that bear live young

which develop in the pouch of the mother. Among the marsupials found in Papua New Guinea are wallabies, cuscuses, tree kangaroos, bandicoots and possums.

Sandy wallabies live in the savannah grass-land of the south coast while the shy forest wallabies live in extensive forests. Cuscuses are slow-moving forest animals, most active at night. They are represented on the 10-toea coin. They are prized for their meat and soft fur, which is used as a decoration by some people, as is the fur of the four kinds of tree kangaroo found in Papua New Guinea.

Bandicoots are common in most parts of Papua New Guinea, but like the small possums, gliders, phascogales, dasyurids or marsupial cats, and other marsupials, they are quite hard to find.

Bats too are common. Flocks of fruit bats can often be seen around the town of Madang, camping in great numbers in the trees during the day and flying to their feeding grounds at night. The smaller, insect-eating bats can often be seen at night around street lights, feeding on insects attracted to the light.

Pigs were introduced to Papua New Guinea many hundreds of years ago and they are very valuable for food and status to village people. Dogs, which were also introduced long ago, are found in most villages and are used for hunting.

Birds

Papua New Guinea has one of the richest and most varied bird faunas in the world. The

most beautiful and famous are the Birds of Paradise. Of the 43 different species in the world, 33 are found in Papua New Guinea, all of which are National Animals. Goura pigeons, the largest pigeons in the world, are also declared National Animals. Because of over-hunting in some areas, goura pigeons have now become rare.

There are three kinds of cassowary, all of which are found in Papua New Guinea. The largest, the double-wattled cassowary, is also found in Australia. The single-wattled and dwarf cassowaries are found only in the north coastal areas and in the mountains of Papua New Guinea. Other bird families are well represented by the kingfishers, parrots and by large and noisy birds such as the comical hornbill.

The New Guinea eagle is the largest flying bird in the country. It is linked in the local legends of many areas with magic, and its feathers often adorn head-dresses worn by important people. These birds could easily be overhunted and have been declared National Animals.

Bird of Paradise (Paradisaea raggaiana)

Reptiles

Representatives of the main groups of reptiles, or scaled animals that lay eggs, are found in Papua New Guinea. Lizards are common and the small insect-eating geckos can be found in most homes. Dragon lizards are often seen outdoors basking in the sun. Goannas, some of which grow to several metres length, are common and their skins are often used on *kundu* drums.

Both marine and freshwater turtles are found in Papua New Guinea. The largest of the marine turtles is the very rare leathery turtle that can grow up to 900 kilograms in weight. Green turtles are a common source of food for coastal people while the shell of the hawksbill turtle, the famous tortoise-shell, is often used for jewellery. Of the freshwater turtles, perhaps the most distinctive is the tube-nosed Fly River turtle which is represented on the five-toea coin.

The freshwater and saltwater crocodiles found in Papua New Guinea are represented on the one-Kina coin. The larger breeding

(Above) Double wattled cassowary (Casuarius casuarius)

(Right) Freshwater crocodile (Crocodylus novaeguineae)

crocodiles of both species are protected by the country's laws from overhunting. Their young are farmed in villages and larger farms in the coastal areas of the country.

Snakes are generally feared by the people of Papua New Guinea. They occur in large numbers in the lowlands and their numbers decrease with altitude. The largest snake in the country is the amethystine python which grows up to seven metres in length. The most beautiful is the D'Albertis. The green python is unusual because the young ones are bright yellow in color but change to the beautiful green color of the adults as they grow. There are several kinds of poisonous snakes in Papua New Guinea including the death adder and taipan.

Brown tree snake (Boiga irregularis)

Frogs

The largest tree-frog, the white-lipped tree frog which grows to 14 centimetres long, is found in Papua New Guinea. The beautiful green tree frogs are common and are easily seen. Ground-living species are also common, as is the introduced cane toad.

Largest green tree frog (Litoria infrafrenata)

Insects

A rich insect fauna exists in Papua New Guinea. Among the most beautiful are the birdwing butterflies of which seven kinds are National Animals. Of these the female Queen Alexandra's Birdwing is the largest butterfly in the world, having a wingspan of up to 25 centimetres. The Paradise Birdwing butterfly is represented on the one-toea coin and the Goliath Birdwing on one of the 100-Kina commemorative coins.

Many large and unusual grasshoppers and stick insects are found in Papua New Guinea as are many beautiful beetles. These are now being farmed and collected, using habitat enrichment with controlled harvesting to ensure conservation.

Butterly (Ornithoptera priamus)

Conservation

Conservation of natural resources is one of the priorities of the Government of Papua New Guinea. The wildlife in this country belongs to the people on whose land it is found. These landowners know much about their animals. They usually have traditional laws to conserve the resources on which they depend.

Today wildlife and habitat are being preserved by the people in several types of conservation areas, one of which is the Wildlife Management Area. The people administer these areas themselves and are responsible for the conservation, management and use of their natural resources.

There are also National Parks and other types of conservation areas in Papua New Guinea, with more being developed all the time. Active co-operation between the people and Government conservation agencies is needed to help conserve and in some cases increase the wildlife resources of the country.

History

Pre-History

People first settled New Guinea and Australia about 50 000 years ago when they formed one land mass. The earliest settlers to New Guinea probably came from the eastern Indonesian islands. They have originated from South-East Asia and crossed land bridges to Indonesia several hundred thousands years ago.

The first New Guineans were hunters and gatherers. They practised an economy similar to that still used by Australian aborigines today.

The first settlers arrived in New Guinea during the glacial period. At that time many of the mountains of New Guinea and other parts of the world were covered with snow and ice. Grassland areas were also wider and contained many animals, providing important hunting grounds for the early settlers.

World climates grew warmer between 17 000 and 10 000 years ago, causing the melting of ice sheets. As a result sea levels began to rise and the land connection between Australia and New Guinea gradually came under water. The last link in Torres Strait disappeared about 8 000 years ago.

From then on separate developments took place in New Guinea and Australia. In New Guinea agriculture became the means of livelihood as forests increased in area.

Agricultural methods and new food crops were probably introduced into the area by farmers who had migrated from South-East Asia. The agricultural economy resulted in bigger populations and fixed settlements. Agricultural communities grew as more farming tools were developed.

Scientists have found evidence that wide areas of the Wahgi Valley swamplands in the Western Highlands were drained of water to make the swamps productive. They concluded that a permanent system of agriculture, with drainage systems and garden tools, was established as early as 5 000 years ago in the area.

The sweet potato was introduced into agricultural areas in the Highlands 1 200 years ago and became the staple crop in several populated centres. It was well accepted since it grew even in relatively poor soil, matured more quickly and produced more yield than most crops grown in high places. The growing of sweet potato allowed settlement and agriculture in areas as high as 2 800 metres.

In lowland agricultural areas old crops, like yam and taro, were as widely grown as the sweet potato of the Highlands and supported equally-populated areas. However no big, complex societies developed from either lowland or highland agriculture in New Guinea during the 6 000 years of its existence. Over the centuries, very sophisticated production methods were developed to extract the maximum yields possible without metal tools.

The ancient societies in the Highlands were probably often at war with each other, as shown by the fighting ditches, trenched roads and defensive gates found in the Southern Highlands. The people lived on hills for protection against enemies. Level valleys were used only for battle.

Despite this fighting, there was trading of sago, pottery, shells, salt and stone axes. Before the first Europeans reached New Guinea, important trade routes existed between the people of the Highlands and those of the Gulf area. The route was the major source of pearl shell, at that time a form of wealth and trade currency in the Highlands.

Large-scale sea-going trade expeditions called "Hiri" were also made by villagers from the Port Moresby area. The Motu people sailed on

big canoes called lakatois and traded their pots for sago and canoe logs in the Gulf area. Port Moresby was thus an important trade centre before the first foreigners arrived. Similar trade networks flourished in and around the Islands and into the Eastern Highlands.

Trading expeditions were not limited only to nearby communities. Records show that nearly 1 000 years ago mainland Papuan slaves from what is now Irian Jaya were used as labour in the building of a temple in Java.

There is also some archaeological evidence of trading links with Asia. Metal goods, glass beads, cloth and Chinese porcelain were favored items with the New Guineans. In return they traded tree bark, spices and bird feathers, particularly the much-valued Bird of Paradise. Chinese merchants and sea captains often acted as middlemen in this trade.

Early Contact with Foreigners

European sea captains and navigators were the first travellers to record their meetings with the people of New Guinea. The first European to reach New Guinea was probably Jorge de Meneses, a Portuguese sea captain. He sighted the New Guinea mainland in 1526 and named it Ilhas dos Papuas, land of frizzy-haired people.

In 1528 Spanish captain Alvaro de Saavedra sighted the northern coastline and the Manus Islands. Another Spaniard, Inigo Ortiz de Retes, also followed the coastline in 1545 and named the island New Guinea because he thought the people resembled those of the Guinea coast in Africa.

Then followed numerous journeys to the islands by seamen from Spain, Holland, England and France. By the second quarter of the 19th century the general outline of the New Guinea mainland was fairly well known. Most of the islands were also charted by a succession of navigators and sea captains.

The navigators who sailed the coasts of New Guinea, however, had limited contacts with the coastal people. The exploration of the mountainous interior did not begin until late in the 19th century.

During the first half of the 19th century, foreign ships were visiting New Guinea in increasingly bigger numbers. Initial meetings between foreigners and local people were sometimes friendly, at other times hostile. In places frequented by ships, the villagers became used to trade and diplomacy and could demand the goods they needed.

Traders and Missionaries

From the 1840s onwards, parts of New Guinea, like Milne Bay and the islands of the Bismarck Archipelago, were becoming recruiting places for blackbirders, or people supplying labourers to plantations in Samoa, Fiji and Australia. The presence of pearls and gold in Milne Bay also attracted many Europeans to the area. Samarai became the commercial capital of the south-eastern coast in the 1880s because of its gold, beche-de-mer and coconut plantations.

New Britain, New Ireland and Manus were also frequented by traders and whalers, who stopped to trade and take on supplies. In the 1870s trading stations were set up by the British and Germans on the Gazelle Peninsula. Several years later, Emme Forsayth, also known as Queen Emma, settled in Kokopo and established coconut plantations. By 1884, when the Germans took possession of New Guinea, copra exportation was already a big business in the Gazelle.

In the northern coast of the mainland the first visitor was the Russian scientist Nicolai Miklouho Maclay who landed his expedition on the Rai Coast in Madang in 1871. The Fly River in the southern coast was explored by the London Missionary Society parties, and then the Italian Luigi D'Albertis in 1876.

As more visitors came, New Guinea began to be known in various parts of the world. Late in the 19th century, a number of European powers who were claiming various areas in Africa, Asia and the Pacific also developed interest in New Guinea. The colonial period in New Guinea followed soon after.

Colonisation

First Holland, as part of the earlier history of trade between Indonesian princes and New Guineans, extended its empire from the Indies into the western part of New Guinea. Then Germany in 1884 stretched its base from Samoa to claim north-eastern New Guinea. In the same year, Britain, largely under pressure from its Australian colonies, annexed the south-eastern part.

Some local communities at first refused to accept foreign rule. The people of Madang and Manus, the Gazelle Peninsula, and the Markham and Sepik river valleys put up various forms of resistance. Opposition to foreign rule often resulted in long and bitter struggles, with the

(Above) British navy Commodore John Erskine reads a proclamation to villagers and a naval detachment from H.M.S. Nelson declaring Papua a protectorate of the British Crown, at Kerepuna, Hood Lagoon c 1884.

(Below) A detachment of armed police on parade in 1912. Sir William Macgregor, Administrator of Papua founded the Papua Armed Constabulary in 1890.

(Above) The Papua Hotel, Port Moresby c 1908 a hotel of this name is still located on the same site.

(Below) A patrol including Mr H.O. Forbes, Captain Musgrave and Mr Lawes and a party of Malays near Port Moresby in 1885.

foreign power winning in the end due to its superior weapons.

Other villages welcomed the new opportunities that had come with colonisation. They were able to trade or gain money from new kinds of goods brought in by foreigners. Young men signed up for recruitment overseas, expecting to see foreign places, meet new people and find wealth.

In German New Guinea, workers continued travelling overseas through the 20th century while Chinese, Javanese, Micronesians and Malays arrived in the territory. In the British colony the law did not allow workers to go overseas and labourers were brought back from Australia.

German New Guinea

The colony acquired by Germany comprised two areas: the north-eastern mainland which was known as Kaiser-Wilhemsland, and the islands to the north and north-east known as the Bismarck Archipelago.

The colony was at first administered by the New Guinea Company. The Company first set up its headquarters at Finschhafen in Morobe, but transferred to Astrolabe Bay in Madang in 1892. The Company established many tobacco plantations in the Astrolabe Bay area, recruiting labourers from the Bismarck Archipelago. It also recruited semi-skilled Chinese from Singapore and Javanese from the Dutch East Indies.

The German Government took over the New Guinea Company in 1899, and moved its headquarters to Herbertshohe (Kokopo) in New Britain. This then became the administrative centre for all German territories in the Pacific. The headquarters was finally transferred to Rabaul in 1910.

German New Guinea was divided into nine administrative districts, each headed by a "Bezirks-Amtmann", equivalent to a district commissioner. The Germans required each village to appoint its headman or "Luluai". The "Luluais" were authorized to collect taxes, settle minor disputes, report major disputes, and see to it the government orders were followed by villagers.

"Tultuls" were apppointed to assist the "Luluais" — their main function was to serve as go-betweens and interpreters.

Remarkable changes took place in New Guinea from 1908-1914, the last six years of German rule. Exports were increasing rapidly as coconut palms on the plantations reached

maturity. A series of scientific expeditions were beginning to penetrate the mainland interior. Most of the territory had been brought under some degree of control and was being administered from a series of district offices and government stations.

In New Ireland, the Germans built not only plantations but also many miles of roads. Many of the major roads which now run the length of the east coast of New Ireland were first laid out by the well-known German Administrator, Baron Bulominski.

Thus, German New Guinea was beginning to progress when World War 1 broke out in 1914. Much of the development was due to the presence of many specialists, like doctors, agriculturalists and engineers, among the German officials and staff.

Papua

The south-eastern portion of New Guinea was declared a British Protectorate in 1884, and became a colony in 1888. At the turn of the century Australia became independent and gradually assumed responsibility for British New Guinea. The Australian Government assumed administration in 1906 and renamed the territory Papua.

Papua was divided into three divisions — western, central and eastern. Each division was administered by a Resident Magistrate. Each village had a village constable, whose duties were similar to those of the "Luluais" in German New Guinea.

When World War 1 broke out, Australian troops invaded German New Guinea. The Germans offered very little resistance and the territory came under an Australian military administration for seven years.

In 1921, the newly formed League of Nations gave Australia a mandate to administer the former German territory, which became known as the Mandated Territory of New Guinea. A separate government for the Mandated Territory, headed by an Administrator was set up by the Australian Government with headquarters at Rabaul.

Thus, after World War 1, Papua and New Guinea were governed by two separate administrations, both controlled from Australia.

Exploration and Development

Exploration was a major part of the work of Sir William MacGregor, Lieutenant-Governor of British New Guinea from 1888 to 1898.

MacGregor explored all the important rivers, reached the central mountain chain and climbed its major peaks, crossed the territory twice, and explored many islands off shore. In spite of his efforts, only a few areas in Papua came under government control.

Most of Papua was explored during the long term of Sir Hubert Murray, Lieutenant-Governor from 1907 to 1940. By 1930, when a base camp was established at Lake Kutubu in the Southern Highlands, Murray was boasting that the whole of Papua had been explored.

Exploration of the Highlands region began in the 1920s following the gold strikes at Wau and Bulolo in Morobe. Gold prospectors and government patrols started penetrating the Highlands during this period. In the 1930s government patrol posts were set up at Kainantu, Bena Bena, Kundiawa and Mount Hagen. One of the biggest and last major patrols before World War II covered the wide area of mountainous country between Mount Hagen, the western border with Indonesia, and the Sepik River.

Little development took place, however, during the three decades before World War II. the governments in Papua and New Guinea were always short of money because Australia then believed that the two territories should support themselves, and thus gave very little assistance.

Money came from taxes and small grants from Australia, but this was enough only to pay government bills. The money went to salaries for patrol officers, clerks and doctors, and to the building of a few schools, hospitals and patrol posts.

The missions helped the government provide education and health services. Many people were trained by the missions as tradesmen, teachers or health workers. Still others became mission workers, and together with police officers served as middlemen between the government and village people.

World War II

With the Japanese invasion in 1942, the two civil administrations in Papua and New Guinea were replaced by a military government known as the Australian New Guinea Administration Unit (ANGAU).

The Japanese occupied most of the New Guinea islands and made Rabaul their head-quarters in the South Pacific area. Japanese troops also invaded the south-eastern coast of Papua and came within sight of Port Moresby

Bitapake war cemetery near Rabaul.

but were driven back by the Allied Forces at Kokoda.

The war years brought many Papuans and New Guineans together for the first time when together they fought as soldiers or worked as labourers. Many worked as carriers or stretcher-bearers, carrying arms and supplies to the battle front and rushing the wounded back to bases for treatment.

World War II Japanese barge in a tunnel near Rabaul.

After the war, the Old League of Nations was replaced by the United Nations Organisation and the Mandated Territory became the Trust Territory of New Guinea. Australia continued administration of the Trust Territory, and decided to govern Papua and New Guinea together. The whole eastern half of New Guinea thus came under the one administration for the first time.

Economic and Political Development

Australia discarded its old policy of insisting that Papua and New Guinea be self-supporting, and considerably increased its aid to the country. The Australian grant reached A$4 million in 1947 and increased steadily in the following years. With money now available, development plans for the country were implemented.

More schools and training institutions were set up to prepare the people in the process of government. The First Legislative Council was established in 1951 with 29 members, three of them nationals. Local government councils were also set up to allow village people to take part in government.

The Legislative Council was abolished in 1964 and replaced by the First House of Assembly, comprising 54 elected members and 10 appointed members. The Second House of Assembly commenced in 1968 with 84 elected members and 10 official members. The number of national elected members rose from 38 in 1964 to 65 in 1968.

In 1971 the Second House of Assembly decided that the country should be known as Papua New Guinea. It also decided that the country be prepared for self-government within the next four years. A constitutional planning committee was set up in 1972 to draft a Constitution for Papua New Guinea.

Elections for the Third House of Assembly were held in 1972 and saw the formation of the first indigenous-controlled Central Government in the country's history. It also saw the emergence of four major political parties – the Pangu Pati, United Party, People's Progress Party and the New Guinea National Party.

Papua New Guinea obtained self-government on 1 October 1973. Full independence came on 16 September 1975 when a new Constitution took effect. A month later, on 10 October, Papua New Guinea became the 142nd member of the United Nations Organisation.

The Third House of Assembly became the First National Parliament after independence under transitional provisions of the Constitution. The first general elections in the Independent State of Papua New Guinea were held in June 1977, with 109 members elected to the National Parliament.

Culture

Languages

Papua New Guinea has approximately 738 vernacular languages. There are two main lingua francae, Melanesian Pidgin and Hiri Motu.

Melanesian Pidgin is widely used in the New Guinea region and in some parts of the Papuan region. The bulk of all communications with the people on the part of the Government, the missions and private business is in Pidgin. Some 500 000 people speak this language.

Having been derived historically from English, Pidgin naturally carries along much of the English influence in its grammatical framework. However, contrary to some misconceptions, it is not broken English. Over the course of a century, Pidgin has developed its own features, as any living language does, from the speech patterns that surround it. This development explains the strong Melanesian flavour of its syntax.

Hiri Motu was the trade language used by the Motu people and their customers during the Hiri trading expeditions to the Gulf of Papua. It was adopted as a lingua franca by the then Armed Native Constabulary of what used to be called British New Guinea (later Papua) and spread well beyond the limits of the Hiri expeditions.

Nevertheless, Hiri Motu did not cease to be a language of commerce and social contact and never became exclusively a police language. Since the amalgamation of the Royal Papuan Constabulary and the New Guinea Police Force in 1946, Motu has largely lost its function in police work. Most Papuan policemen have adopted the use of Pidgin along with the majority of the Force, their New Guinean colleagues.

English, however, is the language of education and higher levels of administration and commerce in Papua New Guinea.

Religion

Numerous and diverse religious beliefs and practices, often based on magic and the atonement of spirits and the observance of taboos, form an integral part of the indigenous culture.

The most important spirits are often those of ancestors but in some areas deities or culture heroes of non-human origin are more important. In other areas the most influential spirits are visualised and represented in art and ceremonies as monstrous or animal-like in form. It is not uncommon to find that, within a single religious system, one spirit is considered more important than others.

The individual's right to his own beliefs and customs is recognised by law. Legislation is directed only to those religious practices which are against the general principles of humanity.

The people are receptive to the evangelistic work of Christian missions and considerable groups are now largely christianised. Even in these areas, however, some traditional magico-religious beliefs and practices persist. Christian missions which operate in the country include the Anglican Church, Baptist Church, Lutheran Church, Roman Catholic Church, United Church, Jehovah's Witnesses, Salvation Army and Seventh-Day Adventists.

Popular Customs

The richness of Papua New Guinea's culture is embodied in the people's traditional lifestyles, legends, festivals, other shows and other practices.

In some areas, a wedding ceremony involves a "bride price" (also called "bride wealth"). Some wealth, foodstuffs, ornaments, valuable items and other goods are collected from the bridegroom's relatives and distributed among the bride's relatives. Often the latter offer small gifts in return. No portion of the "bride price", whether in a traditional or a Westernized marriage, ever goes to the young people as a contribution for helping set up a new household.

Certain taboos are observed when fishing in the rivers of the Jimi area in the Western Highlands. A man must not have intercourse with his wife. He must not eat red pandanus fruit, hibiscus leaves or steamed sweet potato. And he must not tread on pig excreta.

One of the most popular legends is that of the Asaro mudmen. According to this legend, in a tribal war many years ago, men of the Mut tribe were driven into the Asaro River in the Eastern Highlands Province. Later they emerged covered with mud and were taken for evil spirits by their enemies who fled.

Rabaul in the East New Britain Province has two popular festivals. The Frangipani Festival — staged to commemorate the annual blooming of the Frangipani flower — features a float parade, mardi gras and sport events. The Tolai Warwagira Festival, held for two weeks in October or November, consists of "singsings", choir competitions and other cultural events.

The National Capital District holds its Port Moresby Show during the celebration of the birthday of Queen Elizabeth in June. The Show combines "singsings" with agricultural and industrial exhibits, and other modern events.

Another June attraction is the Maborasa Festival in the Madang Province. Besides "sing-sings", the Festival includes choir and string band contests. Madang is famous for its bamboo bands.

In September the main cultural events are the Hiri Moale Festival in Port Moresby and the Eastern and Western Highlands' Province Shows.

The Eastern and Western Highlands Shows were started in the 1960s. There is keen competition amongst local people to compete in the traditional cultural events.

Alternating annually between Goroka and Mt Hagen both Shows are firmly established on international tourist itineraries.

Shows are also held in other provinces, such as the Morobe Show at Lae and the Malangan Festival in New Ireland.

Other interesting traditional practices include the "Tee" in the Enga Province and the "Kula" in the Milne Bay Province.

The "Tee" is an exchange ceremony which is held for two reasons: to repay debts (perhaps incurred two cycles ago by one's father) and to make investments in exchange partners. A pig given to one's father 10 years ago might demand of the son, his successor, two pigs of the same size. A pig is regarded as a mediating

The Hiri Moale Festival commemorates the historical trade between villagers around Port Moresby and people in the Gulf Province. It features canoe races, processions, choirs, string bands, "singsings" and the Hiri Queen contest.

symbol rather than as food. It can heal divisions, settle differences and establish friendships.

The "Kula" Festival is also a ceremonial gift exchange but is a form of alliance which involves two kinds of valuable objects: red shell

necklaces and white armshells that form the customary gift and countergift, respectively. Each gift is handed from one man to another in a series of gift-giving ceremonies that recur annually so that the valuables are kept in continuous circulation around a fixed ring of islands.

Besides being used for ceremonial gift exchanges, decoration and sale, shells have been used traditionally as currency. For example, the "tambu" shell money *(Nassarius callosa)* of New Britain is still used, alongside modern currency, for trading in the local market and also for land payments.

Papua New Guineans portray their rich and artistic culture in personal adornment. A gathering of dancers at the Mt Hagen Show in the highlands or a group of Mekeos from the southern coastal area in full traditional regalia is a spectacular sight indeed.

They make wonderful use of plumage, fur, feathers, shells, animal teeth and bones, heightening attraction and interest to their performances. The use of colour in painting faces and bodies is a more striking sight. The application of ochres, lime, clay and crude strong pigments produce a kaleidoscope of colours.

Development

Traditionally all elements of Papua New Guinea culture worked either directly or indirectly for the satisfaction of human needs.

The production of a carved artifact is a good example. There were strict procedures and taboos involved so that the spirit could reside in the carving. A carver may have had to fast or abstain from eating certain foods.

In some places he could not associate with women as they were considered dangerous to the performance of rituals or magic. The carver sought to make each work a masterpiece. It had to contain the spirit maybe, of a dead ancestor, who was highly respected.

For the carver, and the community, his work had great religious and social significance.

The situation is changing. The traditional role of art in its cultural connection is being undermined. The performance of ritual in daily life is losing its significance in many areas. A carver may not carve only for the traditionally accepted reasons.

He may carve elaborate designs on articles that are primarily intended for sale rather than to decorate ceremonial houses or artifacts.

That culture remains a meaningful part of life in Papua New Guinea is the main responsibility of the Government's National Cultural Council. The functions of the Council include formulating and implementing a programme for the preservation and development of all aspects of culture; establishing national, provincial and local institutions; and promoting the knowledge and appreciation of Papua New Guinea culture by people in other countries.

The Council carries out its functions through six bodies, the National Arts School, the National Museum and Art Gallery, the Institute of Papua New Guinea Studies, the National Theatre Company, the Raun Raun Travelling Theatre, and the Village Arts, a commercial enterprise to promote the sale of artifacts.

Creative Arts

The National Arts School is the national tertiary institution for training in the arts, and was established specifically to meet the needs of contemporary artists in Papua New Guinea.

Foundation-year painting students undertake studies in form, composition, colour and experimentation in various media (for example, acrylics and oils).

Senior painting students pursue a more individual course of studies and have the freedom of time to explore their own direction in painting. Studies include traditional designs, legends and mythologies.

The textile course consists of basic silk screen printing processes and production, batik and tie-dye processes.

Foundation-year graphic courses cover drawing, photography, typography (study of type and letterform), layout, creative lettering, traditional design and design appreciation. The traditional-design research classes make use of the facilities both at the Village Arts and the National Museum and Art Gallery.

Senior graphic courses include specialist areas of photography, illustration, typography and communication.

In three-dimensional studies, students work in the areas of metal sculpture, wood carving, copper beating, jewellery fabrication and ceramics.

Jakupa, national artist, working in the National Art School. (above and opposite).

Metal sculpture students use both oxy-acetylene and arc-welding technique. Most of their materials come from used car yards and garbage dumps.

Wood carving students work alongside expert traditional carvers. This arrangement enables the students to study at first hand the skills and tools used to build house posts, panels and lintels.

Foundation-year Music students study the production and playing of Papua New Guinea instruments and obtain a general knowledge of traditional music. The students use tape archives at the Institute of Papua New Guinea Studies, National Broadcasting Commission, and University of Papua New Guinea Library.

Music plays an important role in the lives of Papua New Guineans, particularly in "singsings" and religious ceremonies. Traditional musical instruments include the "Kuikui-Isung", the "Ocarina", the "Launut" and the "Musical Bow".

The "Kuikui-Isung" is a nose flute from New Hanover in the Bismarck Archipelago.

The "Ocarina" is a globular flute from the Chimbu Province and made of clay. The "Launut" of the New Ireland Province, made from a block of wood, produces animal and bird sounds. The "Musical Bow", from New Britain, is made of a strip of palm with a string of vine or rattan.

General theory of music, notation, arrangements, ensemble and accompaniment, rhythm and harmony are studied at the National Arts School. With western instruments, piano is studied with a second choice of singing, percussion, brass, strings, guitar and flute.

Senior music students follow a course developed from their earlier work with emphasis on ethnomusicology (further work and techniques in collecting and documenting traditional music); more advanced music theory; major study of a western instrument of their choice; creative music and composition from which original works emerge and performance of these compositions.

Preservation

The National Cultural (Preservation) Act of Papua New Guinea seeks to preserve the country's natural history and cultural heritage. The National Museum and Art Gallery is in charge of administering the Act.

In addition, the functions of the National Museum include collection, registration, storage, conservation and display of art, natural history, ethnographic and historical material; dissemination of knowledge of the country's culture and wildlife through the publication of research results; building of a comprehensive library and a documented photographic archive; and negotiation with overseas institutions for the possible return of cultural materials to Papua New Guinea.

The Museum's archaeology department keeps the national file of traditional and archaeological sites and a list of all recorded old village sites and other places such as salt pools and stone axe quarries.

Artifacts which are more than 20 years old cannot be taken out of the country except to recognised overseas museums and only if the Museum already has good examples in its collections. The Museum advises the public not to sell old items to artifact buyers. People who wish to export artifacts must have an export permit and the artifacts must be inspected by the Museum's enforcement officer who has the authority to write our an export permit.

The Museum's natural history department collects and preserves unique wildlife specimens for future study and appreciation. Staff of the department go out into the field to collect and study the birds, mammals and reptiles of various regions. Upon returning, they preserve the animals, register them and store the specimens with the rest of the collection.

Specimens are sent away on loan to other museums for study. Visiting scientists may come to Papua New Guinea to study the animals in the field and then come to the Museum to analyse its specimens.

The Museum's marine biology department collects and identifies local marine shells.

Its education department arranges and organises lectures relating to the school syllabus, arranges visits, prepares publications and screens films for students at educational institutions and for the general public.

The Museum also preserves war relics such as aircraft, vehicles and weapons. Its aviation, maritime and war department features a Lockhead P-38F Lightning aircraft — the only F model in a museum in the world, an Air Niugini DC-3 in its wartime colour scheme, and a Piper Aztec, the second one of its kind to fly in the country.

The Museum has two branches, the Contemporary History Museum at Hohola in Port Moresby, and the J.K. McCarthy Museum at Goroka in the Eastern Highlands Province.

Actually, the museum is not a new concept to Papua New Guineans. In Papua New Guinean society, there are ancestral houses, called "Haus Tambarans", where objects of highly cultural importance are stored for various reasons such as initiation ceremonies, fertility rites or magical purposes.

Documentation

Research is also being carried out into the recording and interpretation of all aspects of traditional Papua New Guinea culture. This is one of the main functions of the Institute of Papua New Guinea Studies.

From such functions flow the Institute's responsibility for the systematic recording of Papua New Guinea music leading to the establishment of a tape and record library of such music. The Institute is also responsible for developing a film-making programme to document local arts and crafts, and a publications programme for cultural information.

All field recordings of traditional music are made in stereo in conformity with international practice. This enables the easier analysis of music and accurately preserves the special setting and performance of the music.

Folklore researches have been conducted and several important collections have been made. Folklore publications cover myths and legends in English, and traditional poetry and folklore material in local languages.

The Institute has also become one of the most important publishers of contemporary writing in the country. It has published several volumes of contemporary poetry, novels, radio plays and discussion papers.

To encourage Papua New Guineans to write, the Institute conducts an annual literary competition. This contest offers prizes for a short story in English by a high school student, a short story in Pidgin by a citizen, an English poem by a tertiary student, a Pidgin play by a citizen, an English radio play or script by a citizen, and a full-length English novel by a citizen.

Dance and Drama

Few Papua New Guineans have had much experience in acting, particularly performing on a stage or handling other acting mechanics such as setting and lighting. However, acting in the form of traditional dancing is as natural as breathing to many Papua New Guineans.

Traditional dances are being featured as a result of the Government's move in the early 1960s to revive the country's cultural heritage.

The development of dance and drama as an important medium for cultural expression is being explored by two major exponents, the National Theatre Company and the Raun Raun Travelling Theatre.

The National Theatre Company aims to produce locally-written plays and also to write and direct its own plays so as to bring live performances to Papua New Guinea audiences. The traditional dances, songs and folk plays are treated as an integral part of the Company's programme.

The Company's repertoire includes play productions, folk plays, puppet shows, contemporary dance production and traditional dances. It has performed not only in various centres of the country but also overseas, including New Zealand, Australia, Tahiti and Britain.

The Company also conducts extra-mural workshops with schools and colleges. Community dance classes are arranged to encourage community participation.

The original function of the Raun Raun Travelling Theatre was to travel with "maket raun", a suggested scheme for taking public services, private sector activities and entertainment to a circuit of large village centres around its base, Goroka. The name, "Raun Raun", embodies the three ideas of "maket raun", theatre in the round and travelling.

One year after its establishment in 1975, Raun Raun undertook several aims. It expects to become a full-time drama school where interested Papua New Guineans may study and perform in a theatre adopted to the special needs of the country.

Raun Raun Theatre seeks to take entertainment to village people in the Highlands of Papua New Guinea and an area totalling six provinces of the country. However, this aim has not prevented it from performing in other countries. It also aims to encourage the development of a network of such groups on a smaller scale and to the extent that the Papua New Guinea population and environment can support a travelling theatre.

Human Resources

Population

In 1971 the National Census showed that the total population of Papua New Guinea was 2.4 million. Estimates put the 1979 population at 2.8 million. Based on the numbers of births and deaths each year since 1971, it is estimated the total population will double to 5.25 million by the year 1996. This growth gives Papua New Guinea a population growth rate of about three per cent per year.

In the past, the population grew slowly because of a high infant mortality rate, and the constant threat of disease.

The slow population growth can also be attributed to traditional taboos on intercourse which spaced births two to three years apart, thus limiting the size of a family. Another reason was that many societies practised some methods for preventing unwanted pregnancies mainly abortion, and some infanticide.

Today, with modern health services the population is growing fast in all but isolated areas. Improved public hygiene and immunisation programmes prevent the spread of disease.

Traditional taboos on sexual intercourse are no longer practised and the number of families using modern family planning methods is still relatively small. Only between three per cent and six per cent of women in the child-bearing ages use regular family planning methods provided by family health clinics. There is a much higher initial acceptance rate but the incidence of continuing use drops considerably.

The rapid population growth has had a marked effect on the percentage of population able to contribute to national production; food production and land use; provision of basic education to school-age children; improving health services; health standards of infants and mothers; ability of women to participate equally in development; urbanisation and unemployment; housing and social order.

In urban areas, these effects have given rise to unemployment, housing shortages, poverty, malnutrition, crime and social problems. In rural areas, the problems focus on scarcity of land for food production, malnutrition, land disputes between clans, need for new farming methods to maintain soil equality, loss of forests and soil fertility, and improving the level of services to rural people.

To solve these population problems, the Government has been promoting four policy measures. These include responsible parenthood; easy access to family planning services; provision of medical services to sterilise consenting women who already have four or five children; and encouraging women to participate in community affairs, a move which is closely linked with responsible parenthood.

Rural Welfare

About 87 per cent of Papua New Guineans live in rural areas in clan or village communities. Government policy is directed at developing rural areas to ensure that people have the chance to improve their well-being through their own efforts. This is reflected in policies for the development of particular sectors, including agriculture, small-scale industry, transport, health and education.

About 22 per cent of expenditure on projects initiated in the National Public Expenditure Plan (NPEP) for 1979 to 1982 is directed at rural welfare projects. These projects are sub-divided into economic opportunities, which include rural businesses, village fisheries, small-scale agriculture and forestry, and development of rural transport infrastructure; rural services, including improvements to rural health, water supplies and sports development; and rural education, which includes both formal primary and non-formal schooling.

However, of the total NPEP project allocations for 1972, 10.1 per cent went to helping less-developed areas, 7 per cent to general welfare, 25 per cent to economic production, and 2.6 per cent to food and nutrition.

A major concern of the Government's development strategy is to ensure that the provision of goods, public and private services, and economic opportunities for rural people are evenly distributed to all areas. The Government recognises that some provinces are disadvantaged and is making special efforts to help these areas.

Because of the Government's concern about disproportionate development in the country, work was undertaken in 1977 aimed at identifying the relative status of all provinces in relation to a number of development indicators based around health, education, land, transport and smallholder agricultural income. By ranking provinces according to those indicators a number of provinces emerged as being below the national average in one or more of these indicators.

The Highlands provinces were found to be most disadvantaged in health and education while the Papuan region was well behind the national average in transportation and small-holder agricultural income. As a result of the identification of these areas of need, a Less-Developed Areas Working Group was established to prepare programmes to improve the development status of identified problem areas.

The projects proposed for the less-developed areas have been orientated towards Area or Integrated Rural Development (IRD) projects. The main concept behind the promotion of IRD projects is that while emphasis may be placed on a particular aspect of development, say a road, consideration should be given to other matters that may be affected by the road. Matters to be considered could include the welfare of the people living along the road and the area's potential for agricultural development.

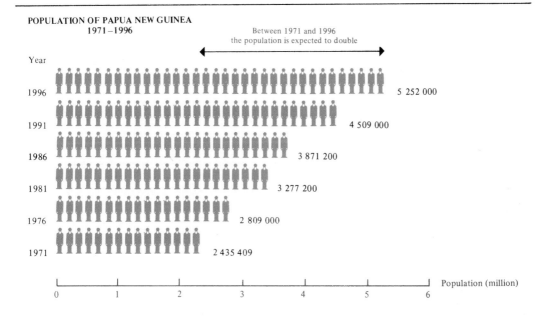

POPULATION OF PAPUA NEW GUINEA
1971–1996

Between 1971 and 1996 the population is expected to double

Year

1996   5 252 000
1991   4 509 000
1986   3 871 200
1981   3 277 200
1976   2 809 000
1971   2 435 409

Population (million)

0   1   2   3   4   5   6

Youth activities and development

In the past, village community life followed a pattern conditioned by tradition and the environment. Little change in the lifestyle had taken place over the centuries. Even when whole groups migrated they lived more or less in the same way in the new location as they did in the old.

The youth of the village were completely integrated into community life. Their education was undertaken by the family and the older people of the tribe. They grew up learning the skills of their forefathers and the legends of their people. In time, they too produced children who followed the same pattern inexorably.

The environment generally maintained the balance of the sexes and the proportion of youth to older people. Ocassionally whole communities were decimated by disease or tribal warfare but in the main essential processes of life maintained the balance.

This balance has been upset. Traditional values have been submerged by foreign influences. Modern science has reduced infant and child mortality and extended the expectancy of life.

Developing countries like Papua New Guinea, whose peoples have been affected by foreign cultures are now faced with tremendous social problems.

An increase in the number of youth in the community; a weakening of their traditional direction; urban drift; a cash economy and many other things have contributed to a national problem of major proportions.

A little over 45 per cent of the population is under 15 years of age. Over 60 per cent is under 25. Only about 30 per cent have ever had any formal schooling. (Bureau of Statistics, 1971 National Census)

Until recently the school system and the voluntary youth organisations have attempted to fill the gap that has been widening between traditional restraints and the freer standards of the modern society.

The colonial administrations did not understand the significance of traditional education. The adults of the time saw the lifestyle of the colonisers they could not hope to attain for themselves but wanted their children to have.

They thought the white man's education would bring the material wealth he appeared to have, so they eagerly sent their children to his schools. Conversion to Christianity also eroded the traditional culture and in fact the churches operated most of the schools prior to the second world war.

After the war, pressures from the United Nations Organisation and a belief that the western way was the right way, encouraged the Administration to step up education and the development of the country's technology so that Papua New Guinea could attain its independence, unfettered by colonial domination.

Although many of the problems were recognised as they developed they were common to other countries in similar stages of development. Indeed, they were apparent in developed countries also. No one had found an answer to them and there was no money to mount massive youth programmes to combat them. Outside and internal pressures were pushing for more and more 'development'.

The National Youth Council was formed in 1978 as an independent body to advise Government on youth policy and programmes. There are 15 members, all experienced in youth work. They are drawn from both voluntary and government agencies.

Provincial Youth Councils have also been established in line with the National Government's policy of decentralisation. They liaise closely with the national body on policy and project co-ordination.

Priority is placed on youth worker training. Strong leadership is seen as essential to the success of youth development programmes. The councils emphasise the importance of projects which train for practical skills appropriate to the community.

Government support is given in the form of grants-in-aid to youth development projects and voluntary organisations that qualify for such assistance.

Examples of youth development projects include fishing, backyard and market gardening, small industries and handcrafts and leadership training courses.

Youth centres are sponsored by government and non-government agencies. They promote vocational skills, community service, cultural activities, sport and academic studies. The Yangpela Didiman (Young Farmers) organisation sponsored by the Lutheran Church, is making significant contributions in this area.

Four international youth organisations are co-operating with Government and the community in promoting youth development.

Architecture student at the University of Technology in Lae.

These are the Young Mens Christian Association (YMCA), the Young Womens Christian Association (YWCA), and the Scout and Girl Guides Associations.

These organisations follow the principles of their international affiliates but have considerably modified their programmes to suit the Papua New Guinea situation.

All of these run training courses for their own leaders and they encourage the participation of other bodies. Service clubs like Rotary and Apex also run courses and offer scholarships to youth workers to advance their knowledge and training.

A number of the churches are involved in active youth programmes within their own congregations. They encourage community oriented activities of a practical and developmental nature.

The international affiliates of these organisations encourage their members to participate in overseas activities with youth from other countries. They also bring representatives of their individual organisations to Papua New Guinea to take part in camps, seminars, conferences, jamborees and other projects.

Unemployed youth and school dropouts have been largely blamed for the increase in crime in urban centres. Some provinces have sought National Government assistance to repatriate unemployed persons and families squatting in their urban centres, back to their own provinces.

The National Government recently allocated K1.5 million to assist the immediate problem in the towns. The Urban Areas Activities Scheme is designed to assist organisations which have feasible proposals to occupy or employ school leavers and unemployed youth. They may apply for grants under the scheme to get their projects going.

Papua New Guinea is a young nation both in its experience and population. Youth are pressing the traditional leadership for change. The student voice from the universities and other tertiary education establishments is becoming more insistent and action groups are formed by young people with increasing frequency. These groups lobbly politicians, government bodies and private enterprise seeking to influence decision making and support for their causes.

The bulk of Papua New Guinea's population lives in the rural areas. The National Government is committed to a policy of maximising development in these areas and it is anxious to see the return of educated youth to village to assist with this development.

High school students in the Manus Province.

Women in the Community

The Nation's Eight Point Plan, introduced prior to Independence, specifically states that there must be a rapid increase in the active and equal participation of women in all types of economic and social activity.

This policy received a tremendous boost in International Women's Year in 1975. During the year, the National Council of Women was formed to encourage and provide opportunities for mutual understanding among women; to speak as the main voice of women and where appropriate present women's views to the Government.

The Council also promotes understanding and exchanges views with similar organisations overseas to present a united front on matters of common concern. The Council co-operates closely with Provincial Women's Councils and other organisations.

The traditional role of women in Papua New Guinea is quite significant. Many 'creator figures' in the culture are female and some societies place emphasis on matrilineal relationships.

Women have always been the traditional gardeners as well as performing their natural maternal role in the family. Whilst the whole family will join to break new ground for cultivation, it was, and often still is, the role of women to plant and tend the crops.

Children would remain with their mothers entirely, often being segregated from the men, except for special occasions, until the boys were considered old enough to join the men's house and learn masculine skills and custom. The girl child would remain with the women to be educated in women's ways.

Women were banned from certain places and could not take part in, or even look upon, certain ceremonies. On the other hand the men were also restricted by taboos in their association with women.

Colonisers saw in these customs a lowering of the status of women in the community. The establishment of women's clubs was encouraged and welfare sections of the administration worked closely with them to promote new skills like sewing and modern hygiene, as well as the traditional ones. In some areas where traditional skills were dying out the women's club was assisted to rejuvenate interest in the artform.

This work has been continued by successive governments and expanded into other areas like nutriton, health care and family planning. The introduction of appropriate technology to rural situations is also encouraged to promote development.

Secretarial training at the Rabaul Secretarial College.

Workshops, conferences, seminars and training courses are organised by government and non-government agencies as well as the women's organisations themselves. A National Workshop for Women was held in 1978 which covered all these areas and introduced training in basic business principles and management.

Girls still seem to be disadvantaged in receiving formal academic education. There has always been some community resistance to girls receiving an 'education'. Their role is considered to be in the home, raising children and tending the gardens and livestock. However, attitudes are changing, especially under the Government's promotion of equal opportunity for women.

School enrolments have always shown a predominance of boys. In 1972 it was 65 per cent to 35 per cent. In 1977 and 1978 this had changed slightly to 62 per cent and 38 per cent respectively. This is a vast improvement on the days, in the not too distant past, when it was unusual to see any girls in schools, but it is still a long way from equality.

Rose Kekedo, a prominent personality in the teaching profession.

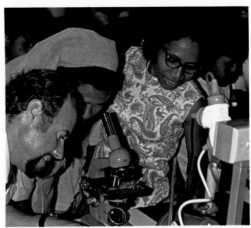

Open day at the University of Papua New Guinea.

Projects such as this poultry raising project at Yarapos Girls High School train young people in the skills of project management.

A student driver learns the skills of tractor driving for agriculture projects.

Many women have benefited from the education system. They have excelled in their chosen careers and reached the highest levels of management. Technical areas still have only a relatively small percentage of women employees except in the traditionally female occupations of nursing and primary school teaching.

There are many women who have not had the advantages of a formal education but nevertheless claimed their rights of equality with men. A number of women in community and business affairs have, through their own initiative, drive and personality attained high positions in the community.

There is no doubt that women have accepted the challenge and are taking the initiative by accepting responsibilities and roles that would have been unthinkable for their mothers and grandmothers.

Traditional arts and crafts are being reintroduced in a new cultural revival. Often these crafts are applied to modern artifacts. An elderly lady teaches the art of basket weaving to a group of girls.

Government:

The Independent State of Papua New Guinea is a parliamentary democracy, with a single legislature known as the National Parliament. The principles of government are expressed in a Constitution which came into force on Independence Day, 16 September 1975.

Constitution

The Constitution has been described as one patterned after other countries' models but primarily considering Papua New Guinea's needs and circumstances. It was drafted by a Constitutional Planning Committee formed in June 1972 by the legislature, then known as the House of Assembly.

The Constitution emphasizes a high quality of leadership, the development of the people rather than of the country, and participation by the people in decision-making at all levels of society. It also gives importance to decentralisation or the distribution of powers at the local level, and co-operation between the executive and the legislature.

The power and authority of the people are vested in, or assumed by the National Government which is made up of three principal arms — the National Parliament, the National Executive and the National Judicial System. In principle, the respective powers and functions of each arm are separate from one another.

Executive government is exercised by the National Executive Council, comprising all the Ministers. The Council is chaired by the Prime Minister, who is selected by the Parliament and officially appointed by the Head of State.

Formal executive power is vested in the Head of State, the Queen of Papua New Guinea.

She is Queen Elizabeth II, Queen of Great Britain and Northern Ireland. However the privileges, functions and powers of the Head of State are assumed by the Governor-General.

Legislative power is vested in the National Parliament which, subject to constitutional laws, has unlimited powers of making laws in Papua New Guinea. The Parliament is a single-chamber legislature consisting at present of 109 elected members. Provision has been made in the Constitution for three nominated members; this is left to the discretion of the governing party.

The administration of justice is vested in a National Justice Administration consisting of the National Judicial System, the Minister for Justice and the law officers of Papua New Guinea. The Judicial System is in turn made up of the Supreme Court, the National Court and lower courts.

The Constitution contains provisions within itself for alteration or addition. A proposed alteration must be supported by a majority of votes in the Parliament.

In accordance with such provisions, the General Constitutional Commission was established in 1978. The purpose of the Commission is to inquire into the working of the Constitution and the Organic Laws and into any other matters of a constitutional nature as the Head of State, acting on advice from Parliament may direct.

The Commission has been visiting the provinces and holding public meetings in main centres and out-stations to gauge people's views on the Constitution. It has also been carrying out a large-scale awareness exercise to educate the people on the Constitution's contents to enable them to make valid suggestions for change where it is felt necessary.

The Commission is expected to table its final recommendations to Parliament in September 1980.

National Parliament

The National Parliament is the supreme law-making body of Papua New Guinea. Members are elected by universal suffrage and normally hold office for five years.

A candidate for election to Parliament must be a citizen at least 25 years of age and must have resided in his area for a certain number of years.

Representation

The Parliament consists of 20 members representing the 19 provinces and the National Capital District, and 89 members from open electorates.

The number of open electorates is determined by the Parliament following its consideration of a report by the Electoral Boundaries Commission. In determining open electorates the Commission has to make sure that all electorates have approximately the same number of people. Each electorate has one elected member in the Parliament.

A provincial electorate includes all open electorates contained within each provincial boundary. Similarly, the National Capital District electorate includes all the open electorates contained in the District.

Elections

General elections to Parliament are held every five years, or earlier if the Parliament so decides by absolute majority vote.

The first general elections for the Independent State of Papua New Guinea were held in June and July 1977. They were conducted under a new electoral law as provided for in the Constitution.

Under the new electoral law, the 'first-past-the-post' system of voting has been introduced. A voter marks only one name on the ballot paper to indicate his choice of candidate.

The previous system, which gave an elector an optional preference by allowing him to mark numbers against each candidate's name, was discarded in favour of the simpler voting procedures.

Sessions and Bills

The Parliament meets at least three times a year and holds sessions for a total of not less than nine weeks. Subject to the Constitution, it may make laws having effect within and outside Papua New Guinea for the peace, order and good government of the country and for the welfare of the people.

Any member of the Parliament may introduce into the legislature a petition, question, bill, resolution or motion in accordance with Standing Orders of the Parliament. All questions before a meeting of the Parliament are decided by majority vote. The quorum for a sitting is one-third the number of seats in the Parliament.

A Speaker and a Deputy Speaker are elected by the Parliament from among its members. The Speaker is responsible for upholding the dignity of the Parliament, maintaining order in it, regulating its proceedings, and administering its affairs.

As in similar legislatures in other countries, the Parliament and its members enjoy certain privileges and immunities. These include freedom of speech, debate and proceedings in the chamber. Members also have freedom from arrest for any act carried out under the Parliament's authority, or for civil debt during meetings of the Parliament.

To ensure full and active participation by backbenchers in the work of the Parliament, there are established several parliamentary committees. These committees cover all major fields of activity of the National Government; membership is spread as widely as practicable among the backbenchers.

National Executive

The National Executive consists of the Head of State and the National Executive Council. Executive government is exercised by all the Ministers acting as members of the National Executive Council.

The Governor-General is the Queen's representative and is the highest ranking official in Papua New Guinea. Under the Constitution he has the power to appoint the Prime Minister and other Ministers, the Chief Justice and senior public servants. He has the power to declare a national emergency or call for general elections. However he exercises all these powers only on the advice of the National Executive Council or some other constitutional authority.

All the Ministers are appointed from Members of the Parliament. Aside from the Prime Minister there are 25 Ministers heading the following Ministries: Primary Industry; Foreign Affairs and Trade; Education; Justice; Environment and Conservation; Health; Media; Police; Defence; Corrective Institutions and Liquor Licensing; Works and Supply; Home Affairs; Finance; Decentralisation; Public Utilities; Labour and Employment; Transport and Civil Aviation; Commerce and Industry; Urban Development; Minerals and Energy; Forests; National Planning and Development; Lands; Science, Culture and Tourism; Youth and Recreation.

Judicial System

Judicial authority is vested in the National Judicial System consisting of the different courts of Papua New Guinea.

The Courts

The Supreme Court is the country's highest court and the final court of appeal. It has the power to review all decisions of the National Court. It also has authority in matters involving the interpretation and application of the Constitution.

The Supreme Court consists of all the judges of the National Court, excluding acting judges. At least three judges must sit together during a hearing of the Court although an Act of Parliament or Rules of Court may order certain classes of cases to be heard by a single judge.

The National Court, the country's second highest court, has unlimited jurisdiction or authority which may be exercised by a single judge. It presently consists of six judges including a Chief Justice and a Deputy Chief Justice.

District Courts and Local Courts are lower courts which have limited powers. These courts are administered by full-time magistrates.

Village Courts have the power to hear simple cases like charges of physical injury or robbery in villages. The magistrates for a Village Court are chosen from among the village people. No legal qualifications are required for their appointment.

The Minister for Justice is responsible for all matters related to the functions of the National Judicial System, as well as the Department of Justice and other legal bodies.

The Department of Justice is headed by the Secretary for Justice, who is responsible for the efficient operation of all its branches. These branches include the State Solicitor's Office, Registrar-General's Branch, Public Curator's Branch, Corrective Institutions Service, Liquor Licensing Commission, and the Offices of the Public Prosecutor and the Public Solicitor.

Other Legal Bodies

There are other auxiliary courts and legal bodies in Papua New Guinea established in accordance with the Constitution. These include the Judicial and Legal Services Commission, the Magisterial Service, Land Courts and the Law Reform Commission.

The Judicial and Legal Services Commission is responsible for the appointment of all judges except the Chief Justice; all magistrates other than those of Village Courts; and the Public Prosecutor and the Public Solicitor. The Commission is headed by the Minister for Justice, and includes the Deputy Chief Justice, the Chief Ombudsman, and a member appointed by the Parliament.

The Magisterial Service consists of a Chief Magistrate, appointed magistrates, and all full-time magistrates. These magistrates administer and run all District and Local Courts.

Land Courts are those established to settle disputes over the ownership of customary lands.

The Law Reform Commission reviews the laws of Papua New Guinea in order to carry out their systematic development and reform. The Commission studies ways of updating, simplifying and adopting new methods for administering laws and dealing out justice. It also recommends new approaches and ideas that will help make these laws suitable to the changing needs of Papua New Guinea.

Public Service

A National Public Service implements policies of the National Executive and carries out other government duties. At 31st December 1978 there were 44 403 national officers and 3 542 expatriates working in the Public Service.

Senior officers of the Public Service are appointed by the National Executive. All public servants are employed under the Public Service (Interim Arrangement) Act.

Personnel administration and management matters within the Public Service are taken care of by the Department of the Public Services Commission. The Commission is independent of any direction or control on personnel matters but may be given general policy guidance by the National Executive Council.

There are two major organisations which look after the welfare of officers in the Public Service. These are the Public Service Association, and the Overseas Staffing Assistance Association.

Ombudsman

There is an Ombudsman Commission which reviews administrative actions and polices the Leadership Code. The Code sets out rules of conduct and ethics for Parliamentarians and senior public servants. Members of the Ombudsman Commission are appointed by the Head of State, acting on the advice of an Ombudsman appointment committee.

Officers of the Commission travel to different parts of the country to find out people's complaints, if any. After studying such complaints, it recommends corrective action where necessary.

The Commission cannot require the Government or its officers to change decisions or adopt new practices. Its powers are limited to giving advice, making reports and recommendations, and informing people what its recommendations are. However, since the Commission is supported by leaders and senior officials of the Government, its recommendations are followed most of the time.

The Commission has no power to question court decisions, policies of Ministers, or rules made by local governments. It has no power also to hear complaints against private companies. Instead it refers persons with such problems to government bodies which have control over private companies.

Provincial Government

A second level of government, known as Provincial Government, has been established throughout the country. Elected Provincial Governments now operate in North Solomons, East New Britain, New Ireland, Eastern Highlands, Manus, Central and Milne Bay Provinces. Interim Provincial Governments (which have not yet had elections) have been established in Simbu, East Sepik, Northern, Gulf, Western, Western Highlands, Southern Highlands, West New Britain, Morobe, Enga, Madang, and West Sepik. The latter provinces were expected to have fully-elected Provincial Government by the end of 1980.

Provincial Government allows the transfer of decision-making and implementation powers from the National Government to representatives of the people in the provinces. It enables the people of the provinces to take part in planning and carry out policies affecting their own development and administration.

The powers and functions of Provincial Governments are set out in an Organic Law passed by the National Parliament in February 1977.

Legislation

Under the Organic Law, Provincial Governments can make laws on such matters as community schools, licensing of mobile traders, liquor sales, public entertainment, housing, cultural centres and sports councils, and the establishment of village courts. The National Parliament cannot make new laws on these matters but has the power to reject provincial laws that it feels are not in the national interest.

In other legislative areas, Provincial Governments share law-making powers with the National Parliament. These concurrent or shared subjects include community and rural development, agriculture and stock, fishing, health, and provincial high schools, and vocation centres. They also include tourism, family and marriage laws, mass media and communications, and the establishment of provincial courts. The National Government retains the right to make laws on these matters. Laws proposed by a Provincial Government which oppose or duplicate national legislation are not valid.

Sources of Funds

Upon establishment, each Provincial Government receives a grant of K50,000 from the National Government to help cover initial costs.

The Provincial Government also receives from the National Government:

- Unconditional grants – The main source of revenue for most provinces, which are given every year. These grants consist of an annual export grant and other grants set aside by the Parliament in the National Budget.
- Conditional Grants – These are for improvement programmes and other agreed development activities.
- Provincial Corporation Development Grant – 50 toea per head of population, plus a K100,000 interest-free loan.
- Salaries for members of the provincial secretariat.

For regular sources of funds, the Provincial Government is given power to impose and collect certain taxes or fees. These include retail sales taxes, entertainment taxes, land taxes, a head tax, and licence fees for mobile trading, liquor sales and gambling.

In addition, the Provincial Government gets back the money from certain taxes or fees collected by the National Government in the province. These include royalties on minerals and other natural resources, vehicle registration fees and drivers' licence fees.

Structure

Each Provincial Government is made up of a provincial legislature and a provincial executive council.

The provincial legislature passes provincial laws and makes policy decisions. The legislature should have a minimum of 15 elected members and may have a few appointed or nominated members.

The provincial executive council exercises executive power in the provinces. The Premier and Deputy Premier are elected by members of the provincial legislature. The Premier, as Chairman of the Executive Council, appoints other members of his council.

The Provincial Government may establish its own provincial secretariat which is subjected to direction from the provincial executive council. The secretariat provides advice and administrative services to the provincial legislature and provincial executive council.

The National Public Service is being de-centralised to allow public servants involved mainly or entirely in Provincial Government functions to be responsible to Provincial Governments, through a senior public servant called the Administrative Secretary. These public servants remain part of the National Public Service.

Local Government

Except where it is modified by Provincial Government, the present system of Local Government will continue. There are at present 167 local government councils including urban councils and special-purpose authorities serving 92 per cent of the population.

Each Local Government Council represents a number of villages and is responsible for administering its own area. The council is responsible for maintaining roads, bridges, buildings, markets, water supplies and other community services. Councils get their funds from tax collection, fees, rates and fines, and National Government grants.

Area Authorities

These were bodies which co-ordinated the work of a number of Local Government Councils and gave advice on the development of provinces. Of the 14 area authorities established since 1972, all have been replaced by Provincial Governments. Area authorities have performed an important role in preparing the provinces for Provincial Governments.

The introduction of Local Government may be said to have occurred before World War II, when various church and Administration councils existed. Some were inaugurated before 1914. All such bodies, however, lacked the statutory basis that was provided for the first time in 1949 by the Papua and New Guinea Act and the Native Local Government Councils Ordinance 1949-50. The latter endowed the councils, with many of the powers previously held by village constables in Papua and village chiefs in New Guinea.

Growth

For a greater part of its history, Papua New Guinea was made up of many villages largely isolated from one another, although in some areas family and economic ties existed between them. Each of these villages was well-organised and had its own set of laws. Village leaders or big men gained their positions through their skills, wisdom or wealth. Decisions of the majority were carried out, with leaders and elders exerting great influence.

Colonisation

Papua New Guinea's isolation was gradually broken down with the arrival of European missionaries and traders in the 18th century. Colonial rule followed. By the end of the 19th century New Guinea island was divided into three separate colonies. The Dutch occupied the western half, the Germans the north-eastern portion, and the British the south-east (Papua). At the turn of the century Australia gained independence from Britain and took over the administration of Papua.

During World War I (1914-1918) Australia annexed German New Guinea and later administered as two independent territories.

This dual administration went on until 1946 when the newly-created United Nations Organisation asked Australia to administer New Guinea as a trust territory.

Australia decided to administer Papua and New Guinea as a single territory and bring them to independence together.

Road to Independence

The resumption of government by the civil administration after World War II and the Australian Government's commitment to administering Papua and New Guinea as a single territory could be considered the first real step to becoming an independent nation.

Few people would have thought when the first combined Legislative Council for Papua and New Guinea was established in 1951, that within 25 years an independent state would be a reality.

One of the three non-official national members of that first Council was to become the Nation's first Governor-General and at that time the first Prime Minister was starting out in a career of journalism.

The Second Legislative Council had an increased Papua New Guinean representation. Six members were elected instead of the previous three, nominated non-official members.

Commodore John Erskine R.N. making a proclamation from the verandah of the mission house at Hanuabada in 1884. The Union Jack was raised before a naval detachment from H.M.S. Nelson and a crowd of villagers.

In 1964 the House of Assembly was formed following recommendations of the United Nations Visiting Mission (1962). Successive elections in 1968 and 1972 increased Papua New Guinean representation in the House to 90 per cent.

Executive responsibility, in embryo, commenced in the first House of Assembly. Departmental Under-Secretaries were appointed by the Administrator to work with departments. Successively upgraded to Assistant Ministerial and Ministerial Members, the first responsible Ministry was established when Michael Somare formed the first coalition 'government' after the 1972 elections.

In 1973 the House of Assembly successfully won self-government from the Australian Administration. Not all powers were transferred initially. But in the succeeding two years virtually all responsibility for the administration of the territories was transferred to the House of Assembly.

Documents granting self-government in 1973 are signed by Chief Minister Somare and Australian Administrator Johnson.

Papua New Guinea won its independence in the political arena. There was no violence, often predicted by the sceptics, like that which had preceded the birth of many other Third World Nations.

The transition from colonial to home rule was peaceful and ordered. Some may have considered it was accelerated by outside pressure and there is no doubt that Australia was anxious to get rid of the stigma of having a dependent colony.

Independence

The Nation's first Governor-General, Sir John Guise, aptly crystallised the situation at the Independence celebrations as the Australian Flag was lowered for the last time at sunset on 15 September, 1975.

"It is important that the people of Papua New Guinea and the rest of the world realise the spirit in which we are lowering the flag of our colonisers —

After the flag lowering ceremony, the Australian Flag is handed to Governor-General John Guise to return to Australia's Governor-General Kerr (foreground).

We are lowering it, not tearing it down."

Whilst many older Papua New Guineans openly wept as the flag came down at the Hubert Murray Stadium in Port Moresby it was also evident that quite a few hardened Australian eyes were not altogether dry...

. . . but at midnight . . . transformation!

The new Governor-General, Sir John Guise, announced to the world a new nation had been born. Heralded by midnight fireworks, the celebrations continued with traditional dancing, singing, sporting events and carnival. Papua New Guinea embarked on three days of celebrations assisted by the representatives of 34 nations who had come to us to offer their congratulations, their gifts and wish us happiness for the future.

The official ceremonies went off without a hitch. The wind, noticeably absent at the start of the flag raising ceremony, obligingly blew across Independence Hill as the new Nation's flag reached the top of the flagpole.

The national flag of the Independent State of Papua New Guinea is raised on Independence Hill on Independence Day, September 16, 1975.

The swearing-in of Governor-General, Prime Minister, Ministers of State, Chief Justice and Judges took place in glorious sunshine with a backdrop of happy people waving the National Flag.

Prince Charles represented Queen Elizabeth II, Head of State. He officially opened the First National Parliament and took part in the Independence celebrations.

The First National Parliament was in fact the same House as the Third House of Assembly. The Constitutional Assembly had allowed for this transition in its drafting of the Constitution. Similarly, all the laws of pre-independence administration were incorporated into the legal system of the independent state.

In the words of the Preamble to that Constitution:

"WE THE PEOPLE, do now establish this sovereign nation and declare ourselves, under the guiding hands of God, to be the Independent State of Papua New Guinea.

AND WE ASSERT, by virtue of that authority that all power belongs to the people — acting through their duly elected representatives."

In May 1977 the people went to the polls for the first time as an independent nation and elected members of the Second National Parliament. The Right Honourable Michael Somare emerged again as the Prime Minister at the head of a coalition government.

45

Governor-General John Guise makes the Oath of Allegiance and Declaration of Office.

The young smiling face of Independence.

H.R.H. The Prince Charles (centre left foreground) with Governor-General designate John Guise meets traditionally dressed people at the Independence Day celebrations at the Hubert Murray Stadium, Port Moresby.

Prime Minister Michael Somare signs the Declaration of Loyalty at the Independence Day celebrations.

Foreign Policy

The Papua New Guinea Government has adopted "Universalism" as its foreign policy. "Universalism" entails Papua New Guinea being willing and free to enter into friendly relations with all countries, of whatever political ideology, except those countries which practice racist policies. Papua New Guinea intends to remain a non-aligned nation as far as this is possible.

Papua New Guinea, being a young independent nation, needs to be familiar with the doctrines of capitalism, communism, non-alignment, multi-lateral organisations, and regional co-operation.

The country is aware of the ideological and security problems which face the whole world. However, it wishes not to waste its limited resources by becoming involved in international squabbling on these matters.

Through "Universalism" the Government is better able to voice the country's concern openly on important issues such as decolonisation, nuclear-free zones, racism, and matters relating to the new economic order and the arms race.

"Universalism" has enabled Papua New Guinea to have a balanced and tactful approach to many international issues which face the country. Many of the international issues today are quite complex. Such issues therefore warrant research and careful consideration to properly evaluate various options available before arriving at the best possible approach the Government could take.

"Universalism" has enabled the Government to have a balanced approach to many international matters. It does not restrict Papua New Guinea's ability to express its opinion on the world scene.

Papua New Guinea's "Universalism" policy may be reviewed, but only when and if it is in the best interests of the people and the Government.

Countries with which Papua New Guinea has Diplomatic Relations

Australia	Luxembourg
Austria	Malaysia
Argentina	Mexico
Belgium	Mongolia
Canada	Netherlands
Chile	New Zealand
Costa Rica	Norway
Cyprus	Pakistan
Democratic People's Republic of Korea	People's Republic of China
Denmark	Philippines
East Germany	Poland
Egypt	Portugal
Federal Republic of Germany	Republic of Korea
France	Romania
Fiji	Singapore
Finland	Solomon Islands
Ghana	Spain
Greece	Sweden
Holy See (Vatican)	Switzerland
Hungary	Thailand
India	Turkey
Indonesia	Union of Soviet Socialist Republics
Iraq	United Kingdom
Israel	United States of America
Italy	Yugoslavia
Japan	

Entry conditions

Papua New Guinea welcomes tourists and other people who wish to enter the country for business, employment and other authorised purposes.

Like other countries, however, it requires certain conditions to be met before allowing a person to enter. These conditions require the presentation of the following documents: a passport, a visa, vaccination certificates and onward travel ticket(s).

In addition, a person must observe customs and other migration regulations of the Papua New Guinea Government.

Visas

The main conditions for the issue of visas that are common to all applicants are that they must have accommodation available, be not adversely recorded from a security viewpoint, be of good character, and be physically and mentally healthy.

A tourist or any other visitor can obtain a visa to enter and stay in Papua New Guinea for up to two months provided he satisfies the aforementioned conditions. Furthermore, he must have a return ticket or a ticket to a destination beyond Papua New Guinea and authority to enter the country of destination. He must have funds to maintain himself, that is, equivalent to about 300 kina (PNG currency), or will be maintained by relatives. He must not engage in any form of employment whether paid or unpaid. Furthermore, he must satisfy any other conditions that may be imposed on arrival.

A person who wishes to stay longer than two months may be granted a visa valid up to two years in the first instance, provided he satisfies the main conditions. He must also meet the following other requirements: lodge a bond or a maintenance guarantee in an amount determined by Papua New Guinea migration authorities; have employment arranged (in which case the employer arranges a bond); and has no serious health disabilities. A temporary visa may be cancelled at any time.

A visa applicant is required to declare any convictions for criminal offences. Character checks are carried out to enforce this

Visas are obtainable from:

Papua New Guinea High Commission,
97 Endeavour Street,
Canberra, Australian Capital Territory,
Australia.

Papua New Guinea Consulate,
225-233 Clarence Street,
Sydney, New South Wales,
Australia.

Papua New Guinea High Commission,
Courtney Place, Wellington,
New Zealand.

Papua New Guinea Embassy,
3122 Davenport Street,
Washington D.C.,
United States of America.

Papua New Guinea Permanent Mission
to the United Nations,
801 Second Avenue,
New York, New York,
United States of America.

Papua New Guinea Embassy,
Mita Kokusal Building,
Minato-Ku, Tokyo,
Japan.

Papua New Guinea High Commission,
Ratu Sukuna House, Suva,
Fiji.

Papua New Guinea Embassy,
Wisma Metropolitan Building,
Suderman, Kav. 9, Jakarta,
Indonesia.

Papua New Guinea Embassy,
16 Avenue de Tervuerin, Brussels,
Belgium.

Papua New Guinea High Commission,
22 Garrick Street, London,
England.

In countries where there are no Papua New Guinea diplomatic offices, Australian overseas posts issue visas for travel to Papua New Guinea.

It must also be noted that a visa for Australia does not qualify the holder for entry into Papua New Guinea. A separate entry permit is needed.

Vaccinations

Except for transit passengers who do not leave the airport, vaccinations against cholera, smallpox and/or yellow fever are required.

Cholera vaccination is not required from those coming from American Samoa, Australia, Australian Antarctic Territories, Solomon islands, Cook Islands, Fiji, Kiribati (Gilbert Island), Tuvalu, Guam, Lord Howe Island, Nauru, New Caledonia, New Hebrides, New Zealand, Norfolk Island, Society Archipelago, Tonga and Western Samoa. However, travellers must not have been outside these areas for at least six days before arrival in Papua New Guinea and these areas are known to be cholera free.

Smallpox vaccination is not required from those who, immediately before arrival, have stayed uninterruped for at least 14 days in any of the aforementioned areas. However, these areas must be free from smallpox and travellers do not leave the airports in other countries via which they travel to reach Papua New Guinea.

Cholera and smallpox vaccinations are not required for children under one-year old.

Yellow fever vaccination is not required if one arrives within six days after leaving or passing through infected or endemic areas.

The "International Certificates of Vaccination" booklet is issued by health authorities of the country of which a traveller is a national or alien resident. It is signed by the vaccinator and stamped by the proper officers.

A person without valid vaccination certificates, if required, is subject to quarantine for the following periods of incubation, reckoned from the day of departure from the possible place of contact of a listed disease (or until certificates become valid): 5 days, if arriving from a cholera-infected area; 14 days, if arriving from a smallpox-infected area and refusing vaccination on arrival (if accepting, surveillance applies); or 6 days, if arriving from a yellow fever-infected area.

Quarantine expenses are to be charged to the entrant and shall not be borne by the airline or shipping company concerned.

Customs Regulations

A person is allowed to bring in new items worth not more than K200 (K100 for a person under 18 years). These items include radios, tape recorders, tape players, record players (regardless of weight) and other new goods accompanying the passenger.

Articles over one year old may be allowed free admission.

A person (18 years old or older) can also bring in one litre of alcoholic liquor, and 200 cigarette sticks or 250 grams of cigars or tobacco.

A reasonable quantity of perfume is allowed for any passenger.

All animals, including birds, are prohibited entry by air (except from Australia) and are subject to import permit to be obtained before shipment. The permit is issued by the Chief Quarantine Officer (Animals), Department of Primary Industry, Port Moresby. Some breeds of dogs, however, are not allowed at all.

Animals and uncanned foodstuffs of animal origin from countries other than Australia and New Zealand are also prohibited.

Foodstuffs containing New Zealand pig meat must be contained in hermetically-sealed cans and cooked at a temperature not less than 100 degrees Celsius.

There are no restrictions on bringing in foreign currency. It is restricted, however, to take out currency.

Non-residents may take out the amount of currency they brought in.

Arrival and Stay

A person who intends to stay for more than 2 months must apply for registration upon arrival at the airport by presenting himself before an alien registration officer. He must submit a photograph similar to that affixed to his passport.

Exempted from the aforementioned requirement are nationals of Commonwealth countries.

Also exempted from the same requirement are foreign diplomatic representatives or official trade commissioners and their staffs, as well as the wives and minor children of any such representative, commissioner or staff member.

Upon arrival a visitor may be required to pay a minimum deposit of K400.

Malaria risk exists throughout the year in the entire country including urban towns. Protection consists mainly of drug prophylaxis. Travellers should consult their physicians on the type and dose of prophylactic drugs to be taken, and periods during which these drugs should be taken (before arrival in, during stay in, and after departure from malarious areas).

Visa extension may be granted by the Papua

New Guinea Government. Extension applications should be made well in advance of expiry to the Chief Migration Officer, Migration and Citizenship Branch, Department of Foreign Affairs and Trade, Waigani, Port Moresby. Holders of expired visas are prohibited immigrants and may be deported.

Employment

Papua New Guinea has an arrangment that regulates entry of immigrants seeking employment in the country. This arrangement ensures that employment opportunities for Papua New Guineans are not prejudiced by the entry of people from other countries. It does not affect the entry of most skilled people who will contribute to the development of the country or immigrants who were living in Papua New Guinea before the arrangement took effect on 1 May, 1972.

Under the Employment (Training and Regulation) Act an employer in Papua New Guinea may not employ an immigrant in a work category that has been declared prohibited under the Act. An employer may not employ an immigrant who arrived after May 1972 in a work category that has been declared restricted under the Act without the required approval. Employment of such immigrants in restricted categories is subject to conditions (for example, training of Papua New Guineans to replace the immigrant employees) and is for a limited duration. There are, however, special provisions for immigrants whose work category becomes prohibited or restricted after their entry.

If a person applies for an entry permit to work in a prohibited category his application will not be approved. If an applicant wishes to work in a restricted category, a permit will only be issued if his employer first obtains the required approval through the Department of Labour and Industry and the applicant satisfies the requirements for entry.

An immigrant who is employed or accepts employment in a prohibited or restricted category for which he is not eligible, becomes a prohibited immigrant and is liable for prosecution and deportation. Regular inspections are carried out by inspectors under the Act in Papua New Guinea to ensure these requirements are observed.

Pamphlets on the work categories that are now prohibited and restricted and the provisions of the Employment (Training Regulation) Act) are available from permit issuing officers, and the Department of Labour and Industry, P.O. Box 5644, Boroko, Papua New Guinea.

Research

Foreign research workers are welcome in Papua New Guinea provided their work is relevant to the country.

However, the Government of Papua New Guinea is concerned because in recent years certain areas have been over-exposed to research workers with the result that villagers have become irritated with and sometimes resentful of the presence of research workers. Because of this it has become necessary to introduce some degree of control.

Research workers will have to be affiliated in future with some national institutions like the National Museum, the Institute of Papua New Guinea Studies or relevant departments of the University of Papua New Guinea or the University of Technology. In some cases affiliation to a Government department could be more suitable.

This arrangement will ensure that incoming research workers will not duplicate work already done and they will, where possible, fit into the existing research programmes in their field. It will also enable the incoming research worker to draw on the experience and contacts of others who have been working in related fields for some years.

Detailed information relating to the entry of people wishing to undertake research work can be obtained from the Immigration Office of the Department of Foreign Affairs and Trade.

More detailed information regarding entry and customs regulation may be obtained from overseas diplomatic offices listed earlier or the relevant government office in Papua New Guinea.

Citizenship

People who become citizens are given all the rights in the Constitution. They can vote, stand for election, join the Public Service, get equal treatment before all laws and have the right to live in Papua New Guinea and obtain Papua New Guinea protection when travelling overseas.

A non-citizen cannot:

a) Vote in any election for the National Parliament, local government or any other Government body.

b) Become a Member of Parliament, a Local Government Council or any other governing body.

c) Be guaranteed all the rights of citizens.

d) Qualify for certain economic privileges and help which are open to citizens.

e) Have the right to live permanently in Papua New Guinea.

Naturalisation Requirements

To qualify for naturalisation, an applicant must:

a) Have lived continuously in Papua New Guinea for at least eight years. Absences of up to six months are counted as living in Papua New Guinea. Absences longer than 6 months but less than two years count as six month's residence, but the period is unbroken. Absence of more than two years counts as a break in residence.

b) Be of good character. Written character references signed by Papua New Guinea citizens will be needed.

c) Intend to stay in Papua New Guinea for life.

d) Be able to talk and understand Pidgin, Hiri Motu or a Papua New ˙Guinea vernacular language (unless prevented by physical or mental handicap).

e) Respect the customs and culture of Papua New Guinea.

f) Have sufficient means of living to show he or she will not have to be supported from public funds.

g) Know the rights, privileges and duties of citizens.

An applicant for naturalisation must go to the Provincial or District Office. Such office will have the application forms.

Children under 18 years of age may be included on the application form if parents wish them to be naturalised. If the parents do not wish them to be naturalised, the child can elect whether to be naturalised or not, on reaching 18 years of age but before 19 years of age.

Rights and Privileges

Naturalised citizens will have all the rights and privileges of a citizen except:

a) If their land is acquired by the Government in the first five years they will not have a constitutionally-guaranteed right to just compensation.

b) For the first 10 years after Independence, naturalised citizens will not necesarily have all the special benefits provided by law specifically for automatic citizens.

c) Naturalised citizens can never become members of the Citizenship Advisory Committee.

d) After the transitional periods mentioned in (a) and (b), a naturalised citizen has all the rights and privileges of full citizens.

Economy:

Finance

Since Independence, Papua New Guinea has made steady progress towards achieving the Eight National Aims, namely:

- A rapid increase in the proportion of the economy under the control of Papua New Guinean individuals and groups, and in the proportion of personal and property income that goes to Papua New Guineans;
- More equal distribution of economic benefits, including movement toward equalisation of incomes among people and toward equalisation of services among different areas of the country;
- Decentralisation of economic activity, planning and Government spending, with emphasis on agricultural development, village industry, better internal trade, and more spending channelled to local government councils;
- An emphasis on small-scale artisan, service and business activity, relying where possible on typically Papua New Guinean forms of business activity;
- A more self-reliant economy, less dependent for its needs on imported goods and services, and better able to meet the needs of the people through local production.
- An increasing capacity for meeting Government spending needs from locally-raised revenue;
- A rapid increase in the equal and active participation of women in all forms of economic and social activity; and
- Government control and involvement in those sectors of the economy where control is necessary to achieve the desired kind of development.

The contribution of major economic projects to self-reliance has been improved substantially by ensuring that the bulk of wind-fall profits derived from high commodity prices go to the nation. Together with steady growth in internal revenue, this factor has caused the country's dependence on Australian grant aid, as a proportion of total budget revenue, to be reduced from 55 per cent in 1973 to about 36 per cent in 1979.

Government Planning and Expenditure

In October 1976, the Government published a White Paper outlining the National Development Strategy (NDS). The Strategy reviewed the patterns of change in the economy in the years leading up to Independence. The NDS recognised that not all developments have been in line with the Eight Aims.

In drafting the National Development Strategy, it was recognised that it would not be effective unless its broad guidelines could be translated into detailed policies and definite expenditure commitment. Therefore, the National Public Expenditure Plan (NPEP) was introduced to implement the Strategy.

The primary role of the NPEP is to progressively reallocate public expenditure in line with the NDS. The second aim is to set steady sustainable trends in the growth of Government expenditure based on the overall economic framework.

A target growth rate for Government expenditure of three per cent a year in real terms has been estimated as being feasible. This target is extremely modest when the enormous development needs of the country are considered. However, an increase in the target expenditure would mean any of the following: a halt to progress towards fiscal self-reliance; increased deficit spending leading to inflation and balance-of-payment difficulties or increased overseas commercial borrowing leading the Government into debt-servicing problems.

At three per cent a year, the growth of Government expenditure will just keep pace with the rate of population growth. This means that the achievement of the Eight Aims will depend on the redirection of public expenditure towards the areas of greatest need and highest development priorities.

Government Revenue

The National Government obtains its budgetary income from three sources: internal revenue, foreign aid, and loans (both domestic borrowing and foreign loans).

The major components of internal revenue and their relative importance are reflected in the following table.

1979 INTERNAL REVENUE
(Estimated Breakdown)

Category	Amount[a]	Per Cent
Personal income tax	69.0	27.0
Company tax	32.0	12.5
Import duties	46.0	18.0
Excise duties	36.0	14.1
Export tax	7.7	3.0
Dividend withholding tax	3.5	1.4
Mineral Resources Stabilisation Fund[b]	24.9	9.7
Loan redemption and interest payments	8.6	3.3
Others	28.3	11.0
Total	256.0	100.0

(a) in million kina
(b) The Fund component acts as a balancing item to ensure a steady growth in total internal revenue over time. Hence, its relative importance will change from year to year depending upon variations in the expected performance of the other components.

SOURCE: DEPARTMENT OF FINANCE

Taxation

Each of the three levels of Government has certain tax collection powers. The National Government has the widest powers in respect of tax administration and collection, and is responsible for most taxation receipts.

However, both Provincial and Local Governments can impose and collect certain types of taxes as well. Provincial Governments are entitled to collect both sales and land taxes, and certain fees including motor registration fees.

Most Local Government Councils collect an annual poll or head tax (referred to as council tax). If approved by the National Government, Local Government Councils may also collect other types of taxes. For example, the Port Moresby City Council collects an entertainment tax.

Taxes can be broadly classified into two groups: direct and indirect. Direct taxes are paid by individuals or businesses either directly or through an employer, to the Government, and most are related to the wealth of the taxpayer. Indirect taxes, however, are not usually related to a person's level of income but to the amount of goods and services he buys.

As a general rule, direct taxes are levied on individuals or companies; indirect taxes are imposed on transactions that individuals and companies make.

The main direct taxes in Papua New Guinea are the personal income tax and the company tax. A resident taxpayer (individual or company) is taxed on all income, including that derived outside Papua New Guinea. To avoid double taxation where foreign taxes have been paid on income from sources outside Papua New Guinea, a tax credit is allowed equivalent to the lesser of the foreign tax paid, or the PNG tax applicable to such income.

Personal income tax. This tax is levied on the income that a person earns including income received from investments, during each financial year. As of 1 January 1978, the financial year coincides with the calendar year, that is, from January to December.

Every person who earns more than K18 each week or K936 a year is liable to pay income tax. Usually people employed by the Government or private businesses have a certain amount of tax deducted from their pay each time they are paid. This method of paying tax is called the pay-as-you-earn method.

Company tax. This tax applies to companies operating in Papua New Guinea. It represents a percentage levy on company profits.

For companies incorporated in Papua New Guinea, the tax rate is 36½ per cent. For those incorporated outside the country (for example, branches of overseas companies), the tax rate is 48 per cent.

Dividend withholding tax. A 15 per cent tax applies to all dividends remitted overseas.

Head tax. This tax must be paid by all adult members of a community to the Local Government Council. It is very common in less developed countries and all people, regardless of whether they are income earners or not, must pay it.

Often the rule states that adult males must pay more than adult females. The revenue that is raised is used for projects in the council areas for the people's benefit. Some councils, for instance, build roads and aid posts as well as provide other types of services out of council tax collections.

Export tax. Taxes on exports vary, that is, 2½ per cent for agricultural products; 10 per cent for logs; and 5 per cent for other unprocessed items.

The most important indirect taxes in Papua New Guinea are import and excise duties. There are no payroll, capital gains or sales taxes (at national level) in the country.

Import tax. Imported goods — except basic foodstuffs such as rice, sugar, tinned fish, tinned meat and flour — are subject to a 2½ per cent levy.

Some other imports, especially those purchased by richer people, have higher taxes. Duties range up to 50 per cent. For example, motor vehicles are subject to 2½ per cent general levy, and an additional duty which ranges up to 50 per cent.

However, small motorcycles are subject to a duty of 15 per cent only because they are bought by less wealthy people.

Excise tax. This is imposed on local products such as beer and cigarettes.

Foreign Aid

The Eight Aims require that:
- There should be steady progress towards reducing the portion of public expenditure financed from foreign aid; and
- Foreign assistance should be secured on terms which support national planning and development efforts, and which do not distort national priorities.

These requirements mean that foreign aid, like internal revenue, should be used to promote long-term self-reliance.

Australia grant aid. Grants-in-aid by the former administering country still make up the bulk of foreign aid (some 80 per cent) in grant or "budget support" form. This role was reinforced by the signing of the five-year aid agreement with Australia in March 1976, covering the Australian financial years 1976-77 to 1980-81 inclusive.

The agreement provides for a base level of A$180 million in each Australian financial year, with annual top-ups to take account of inflation and other factors. Including these top-ups, annual grants have been as follows:

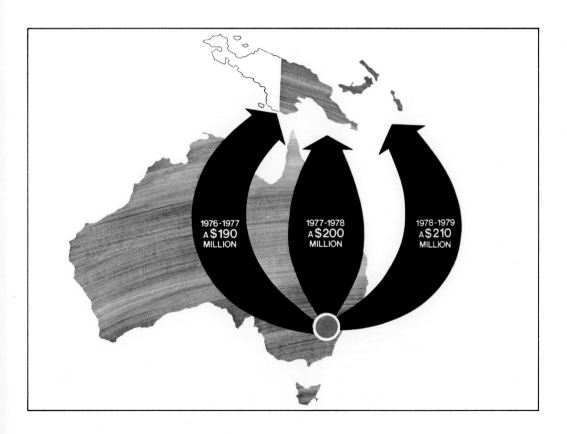

Despite increasing current amounts, these figures imply a reduction in the real value of Australian assistance (that is, in constant prices) over the three years of 7.6 per cent.

Revision to the agreement gave formal effect to a two per cent annual reduction in the real purchasing power of Australian aid. In the medium term, Australia has assured Papua New Guinea that aid will continue beyond 1981 under similar arrangements, with possibly a marginally higher rate of reduction in real aid.

Non-Australian development assistance. Non-Australian aid has accounted for less than 20 per cent of Papua New Guinea's total annual development assistance. However, over 1977 and 1978, considerable attention was given to diversifying external aid sources.

None of the additional assistance available is on the same favourable terms as the untied cash grant to the budget from Australia. However, the Government has developed a framework for using such assistance, which ensures that it can be a valuable supplement to the country's development efforts.

The following table shows loans from major international agencies from 1975 to 1978.

INTERNATIONAL AGENCY LOANS
(in million kina)

Source	1975-76	1976-77	1977*	1978
World Bank for:				
Telecommunications Development	1.70	2.81	–	– –
Power Schemes	4.61	2.22	0.57	0.64
Agricultural Development and Extension	–	–	–	.37
Total	6.31	5.03	0.57	1.01
International Development Association for:				
Agricultural Development and Extension	0.98	0.44	0.21	0.25
Education	–	–	0.34	0.38
Port Development	1.44	0.63	0.51	0.19
Road Development	–	0.89	3.19	3.41
Total	2.42	1.96	4.25	4.23
Asian Development Bank for:				
PNG Development Bank	1.06	1.30	0.22	–
Road Development	0.07	2.86	0.86	4.27
Rural Development	–	0.12	0.01	0.53
Water Supply	–	–	0.07	0.17
Total	1.13	4.28	1.16	4.97
GRAND TOTAL	9.86	11.27	5.98	10.21

* July to December 1977
SOURCE: DEPARTMENT OF FINANCE

Other multilateral sources of development assistance are the United Nations Development Programme (UNDP) and the Commonwealth Fund for Technical Co-operation (CFTC). In addition to New Zealand, bilateral agreements have been reached with Japan, the Federal Republic of Germany, and the European Economic Community. This bilateral aid is in the form of technical assistance, materials and products, rather than budgetary support.

Currency

Papua New Guinea used to have a common currency with Australia. The Australian dollar was used as the major currency unit, with the Australian cent as the minor currency unit.

Papua New Guinea's own currency was first issued on 19 April 1975. However, a dual currency period existed for several months until the end of 1975. During this period, both the Papua New Guinean currency and the Australian money were acceptable as legal tender and were of equal value.

The present major currency unit is called "kina" (pronounced "keena"). It is named after the valuable pearl shell which was used widely in the Highlands and Sepik regions as traditional currency. The minor currency unit is called "toea" (pronounced "toya"), named after an arm shell used widely in coastal Papua for trading and bride-price payments.

Each kina is divided into 100 toea. Coins are in 1, 2, 5, 10 and 20 toea and one kina (K1) denominations. Notes are in K2, K5, K10 and K20 denominations.

Exchange rates. On termination of the dual currency system at the end of December 1975, the exchange rate for the kina was established at parity with the Australian dollar to which it was pegged. Since December 1976, its value has been determined by reference to a "basket" of foreign currencies.

Over the next few years, intermittent adjustments of the exchange rate of the kina were made in terms of the Australian dollar. The objective of adjustments has been to preserve, as far as possible, the kina's value in terms of foreign currencies of importance to Papua New Guinea.

A switch to a policy of daily adjustments of the kina's exchange rates in terms of the Australian dollar was made on 5 June 1978. Papua New Guinea's exchange rates in 1978 reflected the impact of the substantial weakening of the US dollar and the strengthening of the Japanese yen.

Since the kina was first introduced, its value in terms of the "basket" of foreign currencies had risen by just over 7 per cent by mid-1979, whereas it had appreciated against the Australian dollar by 26 per cent.

Exchange control. Exchange control in Papua New Guinea basically means the control by the Bank of Papua New Guinea of all financial transactions between the country's residents and residents of other countries. The Government's exchange control policy seeks to prevent the speculative movement of large sums of money which could have a de-stabilising effect on the economy and the currency.

The four commercial banks act as authorised dealers in foreign exchange. Applications for exchange control approval are normally submitted to an authorised dealer who will assist with completion of any proper application forms. The dealer will also arrange for reference to be made to the Bank of Papua New Guinea where necessary.

Authorised dealers have extensive delegated authority from the Bank of Papua New Guinea to deal with most applications. Approvals of remittances generally have a validity of three months.

Foreign currency is readily made available for all types of current payments such as those for imports and services, royalties, charterage, commissions, etc. No restriction is placed on the remittance of dividends, profits and other earnings (net of tax) due to overseas residents. Approval is also given to the repatriation of overseas-owned capital.

Banking

The banking system, until the early 1970s, was an extension of the Australian banking network. However, major changes have occurred over the past six years aimed at developing a well-rounded banking system to serve the needs of the people. At present there exists a central bank, four commercial banks and a development bank.

Bank of Papua New Guinea. On 1 November 1973, the Bank of Papua New Guinea was established as the country's central bank, shortly before self-government was achieved.

Besides supervising domestic currency operations, the Bank of Papua New Guinea has been administering foreign exchange and managing the country's international reserves. It has also been generally supervising the banking system and administering the activities of savings and loan societies through the Registry of Savings and Loan Societies.

Commercial banks. There are four commercial banks operating throughout the country. Three of these are Australian banks, namely, the Australia and New Zealand Banking Group (PNG) Ltd., the Bank of New South Wales (PNG) Ltd., and the Bank of South Pacific Ltd. The other country-wide bank is the Papua New Guinea Banking Corporation.

The commercial banks have made very strong efforts to widen their representation throughout the country. From 1975 to 1978, the number of full branches and sub-branches nearly doubled to 79, and the number of agencies rose moderately to 358. Their branches are found in all major centres, and banking hours are from 9 a.m. – 2 p.m., Monday to Thursday; and 9 a.m. – 5 p.m., Friday.

Progress has been made towards increased localisation of the banking industry and modification of operational practices to suit conditions in Papua New Guinea.

The commercial banks have been requested by the Bank of Papua New Guinea to give a general preference in their lending to the needs of Papua New Guinean-owned enterprises, and give high priority to financing activities which could boost the export promotion programme.

Papua New Guinea Banking Corporation. As a commercial enterprise wholly owned by the Government, the PNGBC has two primary obligations. It has to be operated on a profitable basis and must foster the achievement of national goals.

The blending of these aims is not always easy because at times the Corporation must pursue activities that are uneconomic in the short term but its presence is needed to bring long term benefits to the country. A good example of this is the mobile education programme conducted in the Highlands during the coffee flush season when PNGBC officers visit villages to explain to the people the benefits of depositing their cash savings in the bank.

Papua New Guinea Development Bank. Bank lending to Papua New Guineans has often been considered too risky as the people do not usually have commercially acceptable forms of security. The inability of Australian commercial banks in the country to provide relatively short-term, medium size loans to Papua New Guineans was one reason for the establishment of the Papua New Guinea Development Bank in 1967.

One main function of the Development Bank is to provide finance either for primary production or for the establishment, development or acquisition of industrial and commercial projects. The PNGBC's tasks include rendering advice and assistance to promote the efficient organisation and conduct of primary production or of business undertakings.

COMMERCIAL BANKS – TOTAL DEPOSITS AND KINA ADVANCES

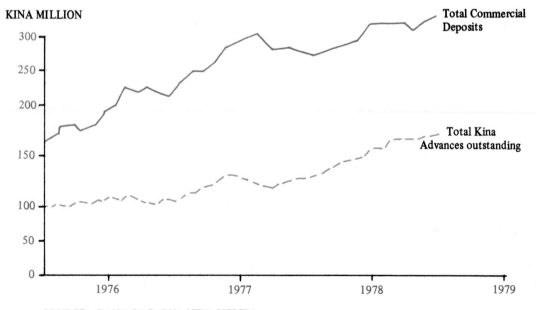

SOURCE: BANK OF PAPUA NEW GUINEA

PAPUA NEW GUINEA DEVELOPMENT BANK
AMOUNT OF LOAN APPROVALS (in thousand kina)

Category	1974-75	1975-76	1976-77	1977*	1978
Agricultural	1 980	2 831	2 267	1 927	6 698
Commercial	4 630	6 295	7 976	4 493	9 667
Industrial	3 581	1 772	1 629	985	1 221
Total	10 191	10 898	11 872	7 405	17 586

PAPUA NEW GUINEA DEVELOPMENT BANK
PERCENTAGE DISTRIBUTION OF LOAN APPROVALS

Category	1974-75	1975-76	1976-77	1977*	1978
Agricultural	19.4	26.0	19.1	26.0	38.1
Commercial	45.4	57.8	67.2	60.7	55.0
Industrial	35.2	16.2	13.7	13.3	6.9
Total	100.0	100.0	100.0	100.0	100.0

* July to December 1977
SOURCE: PAPUA NEW GUINEA DEVELOPMENT BANK

Non-Bank Financial Institutions

Non-bank financial institutions comprise three finance companies, 172 savings and loan societies, and the Investment Corporation of Papua New Guinea.

Finance companies. Their activities include the provision of credit mainly in the form of lease and hire purchase finance. The greater part of this business relates to motor vehicles, machinery and equipment.

The operations of the overseas-owned finance companies were previously financed by their principals. However, they are now offering securities to domestic investors in the form of unsecured term deposits for periods of 3 to 24 months at rates above those of commercial banks. The third finance company is financed mainly through shareholders' funds.

Savings and loan societies. These are essentially credit unions and provide loan finance to their members mainly for consumption, housing and small-scale investment purposes. Their total funds increased from K4 million in 1976 to K22 million in 1978. Membership has nearly doubled to about 100 000 over the same period.

Investment Corporation of Papua New Guinea. The Corporation seeks to increase the proportion of Papua New Guinean equity in enterprises in the country. It invests by direct negotiation generally for around 20 to 30 per cent of company equity which also entitles it to board representation.

Primary Industry

Historically, Papua New Guinea and its people have always relied on the land to provide all the necessities of life. The land is at the root of culture as well as being the source from which the people have squeezed an existence. In most areas this was never easy and in some it was almost impossible.

With a traditional background of land usage and detailed knowledge of their own particular environments it is not surprising therefore that Papua New Guinea still relies heavily on the land to provide most of its needs internally, as well as developing the resource to provide export income.

It is only in the last decade or so that emphasis has swung away from primary products in the agricultural area as the country's major overseas income earner, apart from direct grants from the previous colonial administration.

Primary Industry in this context is concerned mainly with agriculture and stock raising and recent developments of the fish resource. Minerals and forestry are treated separately elsewhere in this publication.

The Land as an agricultural resource

Although the surface area of the country is approximately 470 000 square kilometres only 24 000 of these or about five per cent is considered suitable for high production farming. Grasslands comprise 40 000 sq km and commercial forests another 150 000 sq km.

The rest of the country is made up of rugged mountains, uncommercial forests and land of only marginal fertility and swamps.

Relatively small population concentrations, their isolation from each other through language and terrain, poor or no communication with the outside world and other related factors have all contributed historically to a dependence on the land in a subsistence economy.

Even today the greater percentage of people live in the rural areas and still depend largely on the land for their livelihood. It is not surprising then that agricultural activities dominate the economy. Farmers, subsistence gardeners, fishermen and their families together make up three quarters of the population. Many of the remainder also depend indirectly on agriculture.

Agricultural activity can be broadly divided into two major categories: food production and export crops.

Food Production

Traditional subsistence foods include sweet potato, taro, sago, bananas and a variety of other vegetables, root crops and nuts. Fish are an important part of the diet in coastal areas. Poultry and wild fowl contribute to the protein needs of people in other areas.

Although pigs are raised in considerable numbers they are not generally considered an important food source. The pig has great social significance in the traditional culture. It has considerable standing as a symbol of wealth and may be given away or used on ceremonial occasions to enhance the owners standing in the community.

An introduced crop, pepper is grown in several provinces.

Coffee is a major export crop. (Above) fermented coffee beans are spray washed before drying (below) dried beans are carefully examined and poor quality beans removed.

Thousands may be slaughtered at traditional feasts and the carcases butchered, distributed, and consumed over a wide area. But the practice is primarily social or cultural. Their value as food is secondary.

Only a few new food crops have been accepted by subsistence farmers. Among these are varieties of legumes, maize and a number of vegetables.

As the number of wage earners increases subsistence farmers are growing food surplus to their own requirements and entering the cash economy by selling it in town and rural markets. It is sold direct to the consumer by the producer or his family. It is estimated that about K30 million annually is injected into the rural economy in this way. Coffee is possibly the only other product that brings the small grower a greater cash income.

Replacing food imports. An urban cash economy, a large number of expatriate families in the community and exposure to the 'outside' world in a variety of ways have all contributed to non-traditional foods being imported to Papua New Guinea.

Many of these can be replaced by home grown products and if available in sufficient quantity could reduce appreciably the outflow of cash to foreign countries. The Government has introduced a food import replacement programme aimed at achieving a more self reliant and diversified agricultural economy. This programme has also achieved some initial success in certain sectors.

Table 1 shows the more important of these imports. It can be seen that their value and quantity is quite significant. The total outgoing payments for these imports in 1978 was estimated at K95 million.

Several factors account for these large imports.

- Inadequate production of fish and meat internally.
- Difficulty of transporting and storing unprocessed staple foods.
- Few feeder roads from farms to markets.
- Extremely limited marketing and food processing facilities.
- A rapid increase in urban population.

Table 1

SELECTED FOOD IMPORTS
(Quantity in thousand tonnes; value in million kina)

Commodity	1974-75	1975-76	1978[a]
Rice			
Quantity	54.9	52.4	80
Value	14.4	12.7	17
Canned mackerel			
Quantity	8.4	21.6	25
Value	3.3	7.6	13
Selected canned meat[b]			
Quantity	5.9	6.4	11
Value	6.3	7.5	13
Sugar			
Quantity	19	19.3	23
Value	7.2	6.7	6
Fresh and frozen beef			
Quantity	1.8	2.4	6
Value	1.8	2.0	4

(a)   Preliminary estimate
(b)   Canned beef, meat with cereal, meat with vegetables

SOURCE: BUREAU OF STATISTICS AND
            DEPARTMENT OF PRIMARY INDUSTRY

Major crops for internal use

Beef production to meet local demand has been stimulated by an active extension effort to promote small holder cattle raising. The development of large ranches to be owned by traditonal landholders has recently been investigated and looks promising. A start has been made in buffalo raising.

Cattle numbers are shown in Table 2 and in 1978 the industry supplied about 35 per cent of the country's fresh beef needs.

The pig population is estimated at 1.5 million. As mentioned earlier the pig is more important in social and cultural spheres rather than as a food producer. Probably about 20 000 tonnes of pig meat are produced annually for subsistence food and ceremonies and about 400 tonnes for sale through abbatoirs. About 800 tonnes are imported annually.

Poultry production has progressed steadily towards self-sufficiency in poultry meat and eggs. In 1978 about 2 000 tonnes of poultry meat were produced locally and 2 200 tonnes imported. Egg production is about 1.3 million dozen annually by commercial producers and about 0.5 million dozen by home growers. Imports are 0.3 million dozen per year.

Production of fruit and vegetables sold through local markets earns growers about K30 million annually. The quantity of production amounts to about 200 000 tonnes. Increased production in this area could reduce imports of fruit and vegetables as well as other food such as rice and wheat.

Table 2

BEEF HERD DEVELOPMENT
(in thousands)

Herd Numbers	1970-71	1972-73	1974-75	1976-77	1978
Total	89.6	121.6	133.2	132	128
Owned by nationals	11.8	27.3	35.4	49	46
Numbers Slaughtered					
Total	6.5	10.3	15.0	18.3	16.3
Owned by nationals	–	2.2	3.3	7.1	4.0

The Government has intensified efforts to encourage increased local production of fruit and vegetable crops. Research and extension work on their production is proceeding and the marketing of these products has received particular attention.

A corporation has been established by the National Government to provide wholesale marketing facilities. This corporation has done considerable work to develop trade over long distances to link various growing and consuming areas.

Local Government Councils are building and improving markets, often with financial assistance from the National Government.

Rice is not part of the traditional diet. Although there are alternative starchy foods rice is imported because it is cheap, storable and not bulky.

Rice cultivation has been encouraged and current programmes aim towards a self-sufficiency in this crop. However it is necessary to import considerable quantities of rice and the present figure stands at 80 000 tonnes annually. Only 2 000 tonnes are produced locally.

Rice awaiting harvest at Bubia.

Rice is cultivated on dry land. Efforts to increase rice production have produced disappointing results as the returns to small holders have not been sufficient. Other factors contributing to its mixed reception amongst growers are the farmers' unfamiliarity with the crop and problems faced due to weeds and pests. However the industry is receiving strong encouragement from the Government and proposals have been made for large scale irrigated rice production.

Production of other crops such as maize, sorghum and soy bean for stock food is slowly increasing. A small sugar production proposal is being investigated to enable Papua New Guinea to become self-sufficient in sugar production by the late 1980s.

Sheep raising, bee keeping and tobacco production are also receiving attention to reduce the import of these products. Technical problems, however, are hindering the development of a viable dairy industry.

Experimental rice project at Bubia, Morobe Province.

Harvesting coffee cherries in the Highlands.

Major export crops

The major crops grown for export are, coffee, cocoa, coconuts and palm oil.

Two varieties of coffee are successfully grown, Arabica, a mild high-quality type and Robusta, a lowland variety. About 95 per cent of the coffee grown is Arabica. It is produced in many parts of the Highlands, mainly at altitudes between about 900 and 2 000 metres.

Coffee production has increased rapidly since commercial growing began in the early 1950s. About 46 000 tonnes valued at approximately K107.3 million were exported in 1978.

Cocoa is grown as a sole crop or planted under coconut trees to take advantage of the ideal shade conditions provided by the high canopy of the palms. Cocoa production has developed rapidly, with exports rising from 485 tonnes in 1951-52 to 30 000 tonnes in 1978, valued at K69 million.

Splitting cacao pods to extract the bean.

Plucking tea on a small holder block in the Highlands.

Coconut palms grow in most coastal areas of the mainland and islands. Plantations are concentrated in New Britain, New Ireland, North Solomons, Madang and Milne Bay. Coconuts are an important part of the diet of most coastal people. Other parts of the palm are used in a variety of ways.

For export, coconut meat is extracted and dried to make copra. About one-third of the copra produced is processed in Rabaul, East New Britain, to produce oil and copra meat. Production quantities of the major coconut products and their value to the export market are shown in Tables 3 and 4.

Table 3

PRODUCTION OF MAJOR CASH CROPS
(in tonnes)

Crop	1973-74	1974-75	1975-76	1976-77
Coffee	32 712	36 782	37 091	49 798
Cocoa	28 714	35 508	30 439	28 018
Copra	73 567	95 455	95 593	78 381
Coconut oil	26 806	26 565	30 040	26 103
Copra expeller pellets	13 564	16 472	14 750	14 950
Palm oil	8 706	18 438	27 086	26 884
Palm oil kernels	1 127	1 416	2 046	3 408
Tea	3 965	4 489	4 871	5 875
Rubber	6 127	5 445	4 911	4 730

SOURCE: BUREAU OF STATISTICS

Table 4

EXPORT OF MAJOR CASH CROPS
(in thousand kina)

Crop	1973-74	1974-75	1975-76	1976-77
Coffee	28 847	33 566	42 225	132 619
Cocoa	23 338	40 075	28 614	55 147
Copra	23 672	28 841	11 998	18 827
Coconut oil	13 761	14 284	7 322	11 422
Copra expeller pellets	1 012	1 422	1 798	1 291
Palm oil	2 685	6 786	6 617	8 535
Palm oil kernels	205	253	155	406
Tea	2 601	3 866	3 977	8 022
Rubber	3 563	2 576	2 654	3 317

SOURCE: BUREAU OF STATISTICS

The first commercial oil palm was planted in 1968. Development has been rapid. Exports of oil in 1978 were 32 000 tonnes valued at K12 million. Plantings now being made are expected to boost production to 90 000 tonnes a year within seven years.

The oil palms are grown in nucleus estates surrounded by smallholder blocks. Growers send their fruits to central factories for processing. About two-thirds of fruit production is by smallholders.

Tables 3 and 4 show the annual production and export of the four major cash crops and other important agricultural products.

A close up of the fruit of the oil palm.

A nucleus estate palm oil processing factory in West New Britain (above) and plantation workers sorting fruit (below left). A stand of oil palms (below right).

Rubber was one of the earliest export crops developed in Papua New Guinea. However, due to the decline in world use of natural rubber when plastics were first used as alternatives, rubber production dropped following the general world pattern.

Despite the trend, rubber production was encouraged on a small holder basis. A cash income could still be realised by subsistence farmers by growing rubber as a secondary crop.

In the past, rubber came from large estates. With the decline in estate production and the encouragement of small holder blocks, the small holder share of the export market nearly trebled in the three years to December, 1978.

Present policy is for expansion of the industry following a resurgence of demand for natural rubber and bouyant prices on the world market.

The system of nucleus estates surrounded by smallholdings using central processing factories, successfully implemented in the tea and oil palm industries, is to be encouraged for rubber production also.

Modernisation of processing and new improved plantings enabled Papua New Guinea to export technically specified rubber for the first time in 1979 under the trade name PNGCR.

Rubber latex flows into a mould.

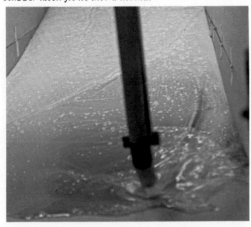

A foam latex rubber block prior to cutting.

Fisheries Resources

The diet of most coastal Papua New Guineans contains a high percentage of fish. Villagers have traditionally exploited the wealth of the reefs and waters that surround the country for food, as well as using shells, corals and other marine life for personal adornment, artifacts for daily use and currency.

Traditional fishing methods were diverse and ingenious. All equipment had to be made by the fisherman from material immediately available from the sea or his land. Some interesting fishing gear has been developed.

Fishing lines were made from vegetable fibres, laboriously rolled together by the women between the hand and the thigh to form a strong string. Nets for catching turtle and dugong were also made of the same material.

Hooks were fashioned from the bone, hard wood and shell. Fish traps took varying forms and sizes in different parts of the country. The gigantic drum shaped cane basket traps of the Tolais, used in the bays and open waters near Rabaul, contrast sharply with the small bell shaped traps used in the rivers and estuaries of the Gulf Province.

A special multi-pronged arrow was developed and together with bone tipped spears were used for shallow clear water fishing.

A Biami villager fishing with bow and fish spear.

The traditional fisherman was dependent on his canoe whenever he wanted to get out amongst the 'big ones'. Canoes also varied in design using a single or double outrigger for stability in the open sea or shaped from a simple hollowed log on the slow flowing rivers. These canoes are still used by village fishermen and the canoe maker is a respected and important person in the community. In some areas personal designs decorate a canoe so the craftsman who built it can be readily identified.

Some specialised fishing could only be undertaken successfully after careful preparation. The fishing tackle used had to be correct but strict personal preparation of mind and body had to be followed also. The 'shark callers' of New Ireland still go out in their canoes, many kilometres from land, and attract sharks by the rattle of a bunch of certain bush nuts in the water. Attracted by the noise or disturbance, and the 'power' of the fisherman, the shark is caught as it comes alongside in a specially designed hoop made of cane. Hauled out of the water, it is quickly killed with a club before it can bite the fisherman. A few older men still practise shark fishing in this way but the art is dying out.

Kite fishing in the Milne Bay Province may still be seen occasionally. A kite, originally made of pandanus leaf and cane was flown out over the sea from the land or a canoe with a ball of cobweb as bait dangling from it. As the bait dips in and out the waves with the motion of the kite above, garfish are attracted to it.

A cane basket fish trap from the East New Britain Province is lowered into position from a canoe.

Their teeth are enmeshed in the web and it is pulled in for the fisherman's dinner.

It is no wonder that such a rich resource is being developed to provide export income. International negotiations have recently led to many maritime nations establishing a 200 mile zone around their shores within which marine resources such as fish, can be exploited with exclusive rights.

This has meant that the potential wealth that exists close to small island nations has now been significantly increased. Many newly independent nations in the Pacific Region campaigned strongly for introduction of the 200 mile zone. Papua New Guinea was no exception and introduced legislation into the Parliament in 1978 ratifying the international agreement.

Fisheries policy

It is realised that it will be some time before this resource can be fully utilised. Following the legislation the Government allowed fishing vessels from Japan to enter the 200 mile zone and fish for tuna and other pelagic fishes after the payment of a fee based on the estimated catch. The agreement ran out in December 1978 and negotiations have been held to renew it. At time of writing these have not been concluded.

The Government has established a strong fisheries policy and is determined that development of the fish resource will take place in such a way that local participation in the industry will be at a maximum.

To ensure this, Provincial Fisheries Councils have been set up and a National Fisheries Board have been established. In encouraging investment in the fishing industry, the Government requires investors establishing companies in Papua New Guinea to train Papua New Guineans in both technical and administrative skills. In the long term the companies will eventually be run by Papua New Guineans.

The Government is in no hurry to rush into agreements with foreign countries who wish to develop any of the country's resources. Learning from many developing nations that have been exploited by foreign companies the Government is prepared to wait to negotiate favourable terms with investors.

Development of Fisheries

Papua New Guinea is one of the world's largest skipjack tuna producing countries.

Japan and the United States of America are the only two countries that consistently exceed production from these waters.

Tuna fishing is centred in the Islands Provinces around Manus, New Ireland and Rabaul in the East New Britain Province. Significant yellowfin and skipjack tuna stocks exist in many other coastal regions. In particular near Kupiano (Central Province) and off the Madang, North Solomons, West New Britain and Milne Bay Provinces.

Skipjack tuna fishing off the New Ireland coast.

The tuna are caught by pole and line fishing vessels. Purse seine fishing for tuna has been tried but due to the outstanding baitfish resources of Papua New Guinea pole and line fishing has been found to be more profitable so far.

Several overseas groups have established Papua New Guinea registered companies with considerable local equity. They have contracts to fish for tuna. In addition, foreign vessels (primarily Japanese long liner) catch up to 50 000 tonnes per year. The allowable catch is negotiated between the National Government and the government of the nation from which the boats come.

A National Fishing Company is shortly to be established to place more of the means of fish production in Papua New Guinean hands.

The only tuna processing plant so far built is a Katsuoboshi factory in New Ireland. However plans are well advanced to establish a joint venture to process 20 000 tonnes of tuna per year in the Manus/New Ireland area.

There are other major commercial fisheries on prawns, barramundi and lobster stocks. This is all centred in the shallow Gulf of Papua.

Prawn fishing is largely carried out by 3 Port Moresby based Japanese companies operating 150-tonne prawn trawlers. A number of other operators use small vessels in the same area.

Lobsters are also caught by the prawn trawlers starting in September each year. Processing plants for prawns, lobster and trawl 'trash fish' and other products are planned for Yule Island in the Central Province and Baimuru in the Gulf Province. The only established processing plant for such products is in Daru in the Western Province.

Daru is also the centre of the barramundi, or giant freshwater perch fishery. They are caught in the sea, rivers and estuaries during their migration. Both village fishermen and commercial operators fish for barramundi which is also processed (filleted and frozen) at Daru.

Minor fishery products include trout, pearls, sea cucumber (beche-de-mer), trochus and green snail shells, giant clam, precious shells and corals and shark products.

Pearl culture is carried on near Samarai in the Milne Bay Province using both the gold and black lip pearl oyster and the butterfly shell *(Pteria penguin)*. High quality half pearls are the main product but some spherical pearls are produced.

Trochus and green snail are gathered by villagers and exported for mother-of-pearl products. The precious shell business centres on Rabaul and black coral, which is only marginally exploited, abounds on the extensive reef systems close by.

Highlands streams, stocked in the early 1970s, abound with rainbow trout. There is one trout farm and a number of hatcheries. Some pond culture of tilapia and carp exists and there are plans to expand the freshwater fishery sector.

Development and Research

As mentioned previously the National Government together with affected provincial governments are very conscious of the need for a strong fisheries policy. This includes provision for research and training of Papua New Guineans to develop the resource and operate the industries that arise from it.

A National Fisheries College has been established at Kavieng in the New Ireland Province. Training and research is also carried on in the University of Papua New Guinea, the University of Technology and in the Fisheries Division of the Department of Primary Industry. Fishing companies established in Papua New Guinea also play an important role in this area and in fact are required, under the terms of their contracts, to actively and strongly promote the advancement of Papua New Guinea within their organisations.

The National Government encourages the formation of joint ventures with foreign fishing vessel operators or fish processing companies. However, it realises its responsibility to generations yet unborn. It does not wish to leave a legacy of badly negotiated agreements or poorly managed or depleted resources, even though the resources may be renewable.

Perhaps the greatest of Papua New Guinea's fishery resources remains virtually untapped. These are the in-shore coastal fisheries of the thousands of coral reefs and mangrove swamp

Barramundi fisherman from the Gulf Province with catch and fishing spear.

73

systems. They are also the most difficult to develop.

The subsistence village fisherman lacks modern fishing gear and the knowledge and equipment for preservation. Transport to market and actual marketing opportunities are presently minimal and in need of development.

The Government is committed to developing the coastal fisheries and plans are well under way to establish a series of coastal fishery stations to service future local entrepreneurs and larger commercial fishing enterprises in this sector.

The future of the fishing industry is undoubtedly bright. Further investment by the private sector is needed for additional processing facilities. It is also needed in the small boat building and ship repair industries. Utilisation of under-exploited species and investment in coastal fisheries development is also needed.

Forestry

The Papua New Guinea land mass is approximately 47 million hectares of which about 40 million hectares are covered with forests. Twenty four million hectares are considered suitable for agricultural use and the remaining area is classified as swamps, waters, grasslands and commercially unproductive savannah forests.

A wide diversity of species exists, with some 200 tree types represented largely in the lowland rain forest and passing with altitude through *Araucaria* forest to the *Fagaceae* and *Nothofagus* forest of the Highlands.

The extent of forest resources has been the subject of survey over a long period. A total area of 4.9 million hectares has been assessed to date. Most of this has been covered in the period since 1964 when helicopter assessment techniques were introduced.

The rate of assessment of new areas has now been reduced due to the need for more detailed information on operational areas. The total area considered likely to have commercial potential is estimated at between 12 and 14 million hectares.

The total volume of timber available in the areas presently considered as suitable for development is in excess of 90 million cubic metres.

The following tables show the extent of the forest resources in Papua New Guinea when compared to its principal competitors in South East Asia — Indonesia, Malaysia and the Philippines — countries which together contribute almost 96 per cent of hardwood trade in South East Asia.

OPERABLE FOREST AREA

Country	Total (Million of Hectares)	Percentage Contribution	Per Capita (Hectares)
Indonesia	42	48	.3
Papua New Guinea	15	17	7.5
Malaysia	19	22	1.7
Philippines	11	13	.3

OPERABLE VOLUME

Country	Total (Million of Cubic Metres)	Percentage Contribution of S.E. Asian Timber	Per Capita (Cubic Metres)
Indonesia	5 200	49	44
Papua New Guinea	1 480	13	627
Malaysia	2 100	20	190
Philippines	1 888	18	50

Traditional timber getting — cutting down a tree for a canoe in the Milne Bay Province.

Transporting logs by water at Bulolo in the Morobe Province.

A major point of importance from the preceding tables is the extremely high Papua New Guinean per capita figures compared to its South East Asian competitors. This means there is no general movement for early liquidation of forest resources for agricultural purposes. The resource base for long-term integrated forest industries is thus secure.

Forest Products

The forests of Papua New Guinea contain a large variety of species of different characteristics. Many of these are already acceptable for sawing or veneer on international markets.

Although Papua New Guinea forests carry somewhat less volume per hectare of commercial timber than do the forests of South East Asian countries, the timber resources of Papua New Guinea have considerable commercial potential. Markets can be supplied from Papua New Guinea forests with eminently satisfactory substitutes for all the well known South East Asian and African species of equal or better application.

Papua New Guinea has many timber species (such as rosewood, walnut, calophyllum, etc) suitable for furniture veneer and cabinet work slicing and many others suitable for rotary peeling for fancy face veneers, as well as core veneers. Speciality timbers of unique characteristics are available for the discriminating buyer for virtually all known end uses.

A comprehensive knowledge of Papua New Guinea timbers exists in published form. Information on strength and preservative properties, seasoning characteristics and major end uses is available. Drying schedules for some timbers are also available.

Timber Industry

The timber industry of Papua New Guinea has the potential for becoming one of the mainstays of the country's economy, both as a major foreign exchange earner and as a key source of revenue for the Government.

There have been marked developments in the industry over the past 30 years. Exports of forest products have expanded from a value of K257 000 in 1951-52 to about K23.9 million in 1978. Royalty collected from timber operations has risen from K208 000 in 1958-59 to about K2.1 million in 1978.

At present, there are in operation about 90 sawmills, one plywood mill, three veneer

A wood chip mill in the Madang Province.

mills and one woodchip mill. The wood processing industry is composed of 130 factories (sawmills, joineries, furniture factories, etc.), employing some 4 000 people. Wages total K5 million per year. Investment totals K30 million in land, buildings and plant.

The industry currently earns about K24 million in exports, about four per cent of total national export earnings. The major markets for these forest products are Japan, Australia and New Zealand. Korea, Taiwan, Holland, the United Kingdom and several other countries are becoming more interested in Papua New Guinea's timber products.

On the domestic front, the timber industry makes significant savings on imports of building materials. A total of 86 000 cubic metres of sawn timber and about 9 600 cubic metres of plywood were used locally in 1977, with a value of about K12 million.

Logging operation in the West Sepik Province.

1978 FOREST PRODUCT EXPORTS

Commodity	Quantity ('000M³)	Value (K'000)	Percentage of Total Value
Logs	443.6	11 890.7	49.7
Sawn Timber	32.4	3 406.2	14.2
Woodchips	114.9*	5 447.6	22.7
Plywood	5.3	1 988.1	8.3
Veneer	2.0	213.5	.9
Chopsticks	3.1	526.4	2.2
Sandalwood	68†	34.0	.1
Other	8.3	434.0	1.8
TOTAL VALUE		23 940.5	100.0

* Dry Tonnes, not cubic metres
† Tonnes, not cubic metres
TOTAL SUBJECT TO ROUNDING ERRORS.

SOURCE: OFFICE OF FORESTS

LOGS HARVESTED UNDER THE AUTHORITY OF PERMITS AND LICENCES BETWEEN 1950 AND 1978 (FIGURES REPRESENT CUBIC METRES)

Year	Conifer	Non-Conifer	Total
1950-51	–	–	24 000
1 2	17 000	30 000	47 000
2 3	23 000	28 000	51 000
3 4	35 000	41 000	76 000
4 5	61 000	56 000	117 000
5 6	60 000	73 000	133 000
6 7	53 000	70 000	122 000
7 8	48 000	74 000	122 000
8 9	44 000	78 000	121 000
9 60	43 000	86 000	129 000
1960-61	46 000	109 000	155 000
1 2	47 000	113 000	160 000
2 3	40 000	143 000	183 000
3 4	51 000	173 000	223 000
4 5	51 000	206 000	257 000
5 6	55 000	269 000	324 000
6 7	65 000	306 000	372 000
7 8	73 000	348 000	421 000
8 9	71 000	332 000	404 000
9 70	71 000	444 000	515 000
1970-71	75 000	656 000	731 000
1 2	76 000	794 000	870 000
2 3	48 000	650 000	699 000
3 4	66 000	917 000	983 000
4 5	75 000	729 000	804 000
1975-76	70 000	848 000	918 000
TOTAL	1 364 000	7 573 000	8 961 000
1976	80 900	929 500	1 010 400
1977	85 900	878 500	964 500
1978	92 700	801 300	894 000
TOTAL	259 500	2 609 300	2 868 900

SOURCE: OFFICE OF FORESTS

Forestry Policy

The major aims of Papua New Guinea's policy for the development of forest resources is contained in the National Goals and Directive Principles set out in the Constitution, in the Eight Aims, and in the National Development Strategy.

The Constitution requires that Papua New Guinea's natural resources be conserved and used for the collective benefit of all Papua New Guineans and be replenished for the benefit of

future generations. It also calls for:

- Wise use to be made of natural resources in the interests of the development of Papua New Guinea and in trust for future generations;
- The conservation and replenishment for the benefit of the people of Papua New Guinea and posterity of the environment and its sacred scenic and historical qualities; and
- All necessary steps to be taken to give adequate protection to flora and fauna.

The Constitution also requires "strict control of foreign investment capital and wise assessment of foreign ideas and values so that these will be subordinate to the goal of national sovereignty and self-reliance, and in particular for the entry of foreign capital to be geared to internal social and economic policies and to the integrity of the nation and people".

These principles are further developed by the Eight Aims and the National Development Strategy which emphasise that:

- The development of Papua New Guinea must be closely related to the rural-based activities;
- Opportunities for wage and self-employment in the rural sector of the economy must be expanded;

- Natural resources must be used to generate revenue which will enable the Government to achieve its other objectives; and
- The benefits of development must be distributed as widely as possible.

Accordingly, the vast timber resources of Papua New Guinea must be used for the benefit of the nation in accordance with the afore-mentioned principles. With this in view, and because the export segment of the forest industry has undergone marked changes over the past few years due largely to changes in international market conditions, the Government forest policy has been revised.

The major thrust of the revised policy is directed at the forest industry making a meaningful contribution to national developmental objectives relating to revenue generation, national ownership, regional economic development and political stability. To meet these developmental goals, it is proposed that the National Government will concentrate its efforts over the next few years in seeing to the efficient utilisation of existing (and firmly proposed) timber processing capacity, and on the formation of a number of Papua New Guinean owned export logging enterprises.

Forestry Legislation

Current laws of Papua New Guinea relating to forestry are contained in the Forestry Act (Amalgamated) 1973, and the Forestry (Private Dealings) Act 1973. These Acts place the responsibility of conservation and management of forests under the Minister for Forests, through the Office of Forests, in the Department of Primary Industry. These Acts, together with their subsidiary regulations, form the legal basis for the implementation of forest policy.

The forests of Papua New Guinea are owned by the people. Forestry legislation provides for the exploitation of these forests in three ways: Timber Rights Purchase, Native Timber Authority, and Agreement under the Forestry (Private Dealings) Act 1973.

Timber Rights Purchase. This is the method for large-scale exploitation. Under section 9 of the Forestry Act (Amalgamated) 1973, the Government acquires timber rights (the rights of felling, cutting, removing or disposing of the timber) if the customary owners are willing to dispose of the timbers growing on their land. Following a timber rights purchase, a permit or licence to remove timber can then be issued to a concessionaire on agreed terms and conditions including payment of royalties, a portion (25 per cent) of which is handed over to the owners. The remainder of royalties collected goes to the provincial government concerned exclusive of costs of collection.

Native Timber Authority. Under Part IV of the Forestry Regulation (Amalgamated) 1973, forest inspectors are empowered to issue these authorities on payment of a fee of 50 toea to any person to purchase direct from a customary owner.

Agreement under the Forestry (Private Dealings) Act 1973: Under this Act, owners by natural custom of timber can dispose of their timber to any person provided the Minister for Forests is satisfied that the interests of the owners are protected that there is no conflict with the national interest; and prospects for economic development are considered acceptable.

Export Price Control. Under the Export (Control and Valuation) Act 1973, no company can sell products for export priced lower than the 'Proper Export Value'. This term is defined in the Act as "the amount that represents a return for the goods that is, in all circumstances, satisfactory in the national interest of Papua New Guinea".

Besides the overall provision which covers the export of all forest products, export prices are prescribed for products by regulation. Logs and woodchips are currently included as "prescribed goods".

Forestry Bodies

Organisations in Papua New Guinea, which are concerned with the development of forests in the country, include the Office of Forests and the Forest Industries Council of Papua New Guinea.

The Office of Forests, within the Department of Primary Industry, is responsible for the implementation of Government policy in the management and utilisation of forest resources of the country.

The Forest Industries Council, a statutory body funded entirely by the Papua New Guinea timber industry, was established in October 1973 to strengthen the promotion of Papua New Guinea timbers. The Council consists of seven members drawn from industries and three from the Government. The Director of Forests is a member of the Council.

The general powers and functions of the Council include promoting forest industries; stimulating the use of major forest products; formulating, in conjunction with the Office of Forests, standards and grading rules; and carrying out enquiries into any aspects of the industry as found necessary.

The Council's aims are: to promote the interest of the members of wood-using industries in all practical ways; to promote a liaison between the timber industry and the Government in discussing policy and other matters relevant to the development of the industry in the country; and to promote and co-ordinate sales between the buyer and seller.

The Council seeks to diversify overseas markets for Papua New Guinea timber and give technical advice where needed. It also aims to develop the quality of sawn exports by encouraging grading to buyer's specification, and the institution and observation of satisfactory standards of marketing; and improving shipping schedules and freight rates.

Secondary Industry

Papua New Guinea may be considered one of the least industrialised among the developing countries. Industry is highly concentrated in the towns which account for only some 20 per cent of the total population. About 65 per cent of Papua New Guineans still live wholly or partially by subsistence.

In 1967-77, about 19 300 persons were employed in the secondary industry sector, that is, in 735 manufacturing and processing establishments. The contribution of the sector to the Gross Domestic Production is about 11 per cent and the sector's share of the nation's bill for wages and other benefits is about 8½ per cent.

Growth

The growth of industries was rapid in the 1950s and especially in the 1960s. Between 1960-61 and 1970-71, the number of secondary industries rose by 12 per cent a year. During this period those enterprises which were setting up may be regarded as those which 'naturally' accompany an administration with its consequential development of communications and distribution. These included metal fabricating, machinery and motor repairing, ship repairing, aircraft repairing, sawmilling, joineries, bakeries, printing, and manufacture of cement products.

However, in the first six years since 1970-71, the growth in the number of establishments slowed down considerably; the number growing by only six by 1967-77. Typically, around 30 establishments are set up and 30 close down each year.

The cause of the closures are, in general, takeovers and amalgamations. In this recent period, Papua New Guinea was then in transition towards independence and, hence, in a period of uncertainty for investors.

A primary reason for this market change in growth rates probably was that those 'natural' industries had been established and the possibilities for new industries to be immediately viable were not very apparent. The industry potentials that remained unexploited were not obvious or easy to exploit.

Market Situation

As far as manufacturing is concerned, the market is small and fragmented. To a large extent the market is restricted to the urban areas which are not interconnected, except for the Lae-Highlands road network.

The significant majority of the population is still engaged in subsistence cultivation and presents a potential source of demand — one which should increase the current demand of almost every conceivable product many times over. However, this factor is not expected to be a major consideration by companies investing in the near future.

The constraints and potentials related to the processing of Papua New Guinea's resources, especially if they are aimed at export markets, are different from those for manufacturing. One principal constraint is the procurement of markets. For instance, Papua New Guinea timbers are relatively unknown.

Other constraints are, the established sources of supply are difficult to break through, the infrastructure in rural areas is poor due to the terrain and vegetation and often very expensive to establish and the procurement of suitable land is difficult or often obstructed due to the traditional ownership system.

Another factor is the high wage structure. Although probably it does not play a significant part in hindering import-replacement industries, this factor probably prevents competitive exports without Government assistance.

Counterbalancing these constraints is the fact that Papua New Guinea is one of the few large areas left in the world with vast untapped resources.

Manufacturing Output

Between 1970-71 and 1976-77, the number of establishments in the secondary industry sector increased slightly from 729 to 735, while employment rose at an average annual rate of 3.7 per cent.

The average number of employees per establishment went up from 20 in 1970-71 to 26 in 1976-77.

New firms have been established, notably in motor-vehicle body building, sheet metal working, electrical repairing, coffee and cocoa processing, meat and fish processing, printing and electricy generation. A rationalisation of other establishments has also occurred through amalgamations and closures, particularly in general engineering, aircraft repairing, boat building and repairing, bakeries, sawmills and joineries.

Engineering and Metal Industries. The output value of this sector rose by 29 per cent to K940 million in 1976-77. Output increased in excess of 5.1 per cent a year in the early 1970s.

The engineering and metal sector is expected to receive further impetus with the start of production at the Steel Rolling Mill at Port Moresby in the latter part of 1979. The mill is owned by Atlas Steel Pty. Ltd., a subsidiary of Kenmore Investment Pty. Ltd. based in Hong Kong. The mill is expected to have a monthly production capacity of about 1 000 tonnes of steel products including reinforcing bars, wire rods, galvanised wires and annealed wires.

Food, Drink and Tobacco Industries. This sector has been growing in real terms at a more moderate rate. The food-processing industries (for cocoa, coffee and tea in particular) are tied to the output of the primary industry sector.

In recent years the breweries have been

expanding rapidly but it is believed that a steady growth has been reached. In cigarette manufacturing the establishment of a fourth factory in 1979 should provide a significant boost to the industry.

Overall for the sector a minimum growth rate of 2.9 per cent per annum would seem to be a reasonable estimate of output for 1977 to 1979.

Sawmilling and Joinery Industries. There seems to be very little growth in this sector. Output in 1976-77 was K35.9 million. Employment increased by 2.2 per cent per annum between 1970-71 and 1976-77 while the number of establishments declined from 152 to 111.

The current negotiations for the development of the Kapuluk Forest Resource, if successful, should significantly increase the output of this sector in the 1980s, principally through woodchip production. This area on the north coast of the West New Britain Province typifies the productive tropical forest with an estimated 5.8 million cubic metres of logs suitable for sawn timber or veneer and 7.3 million cubic metres of pulpwood.

Other Manufacturing Industries. The sales value of the remaining sectors of secondary industry in 1976-77 was K58.2 million, excluding electricity generation which was a further K35.4 million. Overall employment in the

chemicals and oils industries grew by 13 per cent per year between 1970-71 and 1976-77. After several years with output more or less constant for coconut oil, at around 27 000 tonnes, output rose to 29 088 tonnes in 1978.

The output of palm oil in 1978 was 28 413 tonnes. This level of output was the same as 1976 and 1977, after a period of rapid increase. Production is anticipated to rise further with the expansion at the Hoskins mill, and with the Bialla and Popondetta oil mills starting production in the 1980s.

Employment in the clothing industry grew by 30 per cent a year between 1970-71 and 1975-76. However, due to the cyclical nature of Government purchases, a third of the workforce was laid off during 1976-77. Since then, however, employment has been built up again to meet renewed Government demand.

There are two other industries where comparatively rapid growth in the workforce has occurred between 1970-71 and 1976-77, namely, printing and paper products (by 10 per cent annually) and the miscellaneous category which principally includes electricity-generating establishments (by 12 per cent per year). Recently, the industries in the miscellaneous category — cement, paint, canvas, cordage, furniture and plastic, — have shown only moderate growth in employment. Overall the growth was 7.9 per cent per annum and 1979 is expected to show similar expansion.

SUMMARY OF FACTORY OPERATIONS

	1971-72	1972-73	1973-74	1974-75	1975-76
			number		
Factories —					
Industrial metals, machines & conveyances	354	342	379	348	355
Food, drink and tobacco	126	124	129	122	137
Sawmills and joinery etc.	144	135	133	114	114
All other manufacturing industries	98	101	97	122	153
Total	722	702	738	706	759
Persons employed (a) —					
Nationals (b) — males	13 185	13 211	14 331	14 357	15 286
females	371	469	565	660	670
Other persons — males	2 405	2 175	2 071	1 887	1 921
females	375	343	354	351	351
Total	16 336	16 198	17 321	17 255	18 228
			K'000		
Salaries and wages (c)	23 597	24 844	29 062	36 134	43 758
Value of — output	121 548	138 198	183 303	216 958	274 752
materials used (d)	58 174	62 116	95 693	107 604	132 591
power, fuel and light (e)	4 963	6 648	8 541	16 633	24 352
production (f)	58 411	69 433	79 068	92 721	117 809
land and buildings (g)	46 176	46 672	53 507	55 613	56 133
plant and machinery (h)	73 306	72 708	79 217	99 686	125 897

(a) Average over the whole year, including working proprietors.
(b) Persons who became automatic citizens of Papua New Guinea on Independence Day (16 September 1975).
(c) Excludes drawings of working proprietors.
(d) Includes repairs, replacements and cost of containers.
(e) Includes lubricating oil and water.
(f) Value added to materials by the operations of a factory.
(g) Includes estimated values of rented premises.
(h) Includes estimated values of leased machinery.

SOURCE: BUREAU OF STATISTICS

Prospects

Expansion in the secondary industry sector as a whole has been occurring in the new import-replacing manufacturing industries and, to a lesser extent, in the export-orientated processing industries. This is a pattern which started in the early 1970s and should continue for several more years to come.

The Government is concentrating much effort on the development of enterpreneural ability among nationals. It reserves certain enterprises for development by nationals only. And through its registration procedures it

FACTORY OPERATIONS, BY INDUSTRY GROUP

	1971-72	1972-73	1973-74	1974-75	1975-76
1. Industrial metals, machines and conveyances			number		
Factories	354	342	379	348	355
Employment (a)	5 659	5 402	6 075	6 153	6 603
			K'000		
Salaries and wages (b)	12 124	12 140	14 316	17 031	20 889
Value of – output	39 777	40 118	53 025	62 816	72 451
production	21 580	22 152	27 082	32 335	34 372
2. Food, drink and tobacco			number		
Factories	126	124	129	122	137
Employment (a)	4 086	4 114	4 278	4 170	4 509
			K'000		
Salaries and wages (b)	3 470	3 898	4 784	6 005	8 318
Value of – output	36 234	42 554	54 816	66 039	99 961
production	13 572	17 227	19 719	24 019	36 656
3. Sawmills, joinery etc.			number		
Factories	144	135	133	114	114
Employment (a)	4 276	4 182	4 489	3 887	4 017
			K'000		
Salaries and wages (b)	4 294	4 354	5 135	5 808	6 661
Value of – output	19 072	18 929	22 387	23 581	28 041
production	10 083	10 013	12 282	11 413	12 185
4. All other manufacturing industries			number		
Factories	98	101	97	122	153
Employment (a)	2 315	2 500	2 479	3 045	3 099
			K'000		
Salaries and wages (b)	3 709	4 452	4 827	7 290	7 890
Value of – output	26 465	36 597	53 074	64 522	74 299
production	13 176	20 041	19 985	24 954	34 596
			number		
TOTAL					
Factories	722	702	738	706	759
Employment (a)	16 336	16 198	17 321	17 255	18 228
			K'000		
Salaries and wages (b)	23 597	24 844	29 062	36 134	43 758
Value of – output	121 548	138 198	183 303	216 958	274 752
production	58 411	69 433	79 068	92 721	117 809

(a) Includes working proprietors.   (b) Excludes drawings of working proprietors.

SOURCE: BUREAU OF STATISTICS

---

attempts to ensure that no new expatriate development will prejudice indigeneous enterpreneurs.

Manufacturing industries will continue to play an increasingly important role in the development of Papua New Guinea. With increasing industrial progress, more of Papua New Guinea's vast resources will be tapped for processing in suitable locations throughout the country as well as overseas, thus ensuring the nation's continued development.

Minerals and Energy

Papua New Guinea is a young but rich country in terms of mineral and energy resources. It obtains its largest single revenue from copper mining. It is believed that potential petroleum gas and coal resources will also be developed. Its energy resources are renewable, being derived from forests, agriculture and hydropower.

Aside from copper, Papua New Guinea produces gold and silver. Some manganese has also been produced. Materials which may be mined in the future include nickel, lead, zinc, beach sands, limestone, coal, bauxite and chromite.

Petroleum exploration has been carried on since the 1920s. While there have been some encouraging results, it is unlikely that commercial development of petroleum will begin in the next few years.

Giant trucks at the Panguna copper mine are dwarfed by the mine workings as another blast frees wealth from the ground.

Gold – first discovered in the Milne Bay Province in the 1800s is tested regularly at the Assay Office in Port Moresby.

Copper Mining

In the past, copper sulphide lodes were mined near Port Moresby but production was not extensive. Copper mining took a giant step forward on 1 April 1972 with the start of production of the copper mine at Panguna in the North Solomons Province.

The Panguna mine is owned and operated by Bougainville Copper Ltd., a subsidiary of Australia's Conzinc Riotinto Group and with shareholdings by the Papua New Guinea Government and the public.

Although relatively young in the mining field, Bougainville Copper is now one of the world's largest and most successful mining companies. It exports copper, gold and silver concentrates to several countries including Japan, West Germany, Spain, North America and the People's Republic of China.

Bougainville Copper's earnings should be high for 1979. However, production may decrease in the future as harder ore is mined and head grades decline.

The second major copper mine in Papua New Guinea may be established at Ok Tedi in the Western Province. A decision to go ahead is expected to be made early in 1980.

Copper prospects have been drilled in East New Britain, West New Britain, West Sepik, Eastern Highlands, Milne Bay and Manus. However, while there have been some encouraging results, further mine developments in the next few years are unlikely.

Gold and Silver

Historically, gold has been the main mineral product of Papua New Guinea. Gold mining began with the gold discoveries at Misima and Woodlark Islands in the Milne Bay Province in 1888 and 1895.

Lode workings were established at Wau and Upper Edie Creek and a dredging operation, all within the Morobe Goldfield, during the 1920s and early 1930s. Dredging continued until 1966 and one small lode mine and small-scale alluvial mines are still in operation.

Bougainville Copper produces the largest amount of gold concentrate in the country. Gold has been mined in other provinces, namely, East Sepik, West Sepik, Enga, Chimbu, Western Highlands, Eastern Highlands, Morobe, Northern, Morobe and East New Britain.

Bulk low-grade gold prospects (for example, at Porgera in the Enga Province) are attracting strong interest from exploration companies.

Bougainville Copper also produces silver. The following table shows the company's yearly output of copper, gold and silver, and its income from them.

Small scale gold mining in the highlands.

The Panguna mine of the Bougainville Copper Company is one of the largest open cut copper mines in the world. From the mine site to the generating station that provides power for the project, everything is on a grand scale.

ANNUAL OUTPUT AND INCOME OF BOUGAINVILLE COPPER LTD.

Mined		1972	1973	1974	1975	1976	1977	1978
Ore and Waste								
removed	(millions of tonnes)	46.75	56.65	56.00	56.40	58.54	70.79	79.05
Ore Milled	(millions of tonnes)	21.89	29.14	30.11	31.08	31.21	34.11	38.12
Ore Grade								
Copper		0.76	0.73	0.70	0.64	0.64	0.61	0.60
Gold	(grams/tonne)	0.77	1.03	1.02	0.80	0.87	0.90	0.82
Silver	(grams/tonne)	2.06	1.99	2.12	1.87	1.96	1.86	1.80
Produced								
Concentrate	(dry tonnes)	438 115	650 172	640 818	595 498	596 838	615 665	658 587
Contained Copper	(tonnes)	123 961	182 890	184 088	172 477	176 519	182 291	198 603
Concentrate Grade								
Copper	(per cent)	28.29	28.13	28.73	28.94	29.58	29.61	30.16
Gold	(grams/tonne)	27.25	31.6	32.0	30.5	33.9	36.3	35.5
Silver	(grams/tonne)	69.3	69.0	72.0	71.0	76.1	77.1	79.8
Shipped								
Total Concentrate	(dry tonnes)	434 387	625 227	665 702	586 947	605 793	614 819	640 911
Shipped to								
West Germany		186 827	200 333	221 365	243 534	223 170	198 321	206 806
Japan		209 032	342 878	343 204	250 658	256 406	337 090	326 720
Spain		27 565	35 778	57 368	72 184	58 169	47 019	62 082
Other		10 963	46 238	43 765	20 562	68 048	32 389	45 303
Received								
Net Sales Revenue	(K'000)	95 695	249 048	279 825	184 754	205 349	200 578	223 282
Contribution by								
Copper		75 226	203 422	194 159	117 505	142 021	114 699	120 704
Gold		19 328	43 623	81 417	63 706	59 253	81 282	97 144
Silver		1 141	2 003	4 249	3 543	4 075	4 597	5 434

SOURCE: 1978 ANNUAL REPORT, BOUGAINVILLE COPPER LTD.

Other Minerals

Manganese — Small bodies of manganese oxide have been mined near Rigo in the Central Province.

Nickel — Small showings of nickel sulphides have been found in the upper reaches of the Adau and Domara Rivers in the Northern Province.

Lead and Zinc — Occurrence of these metals have been reported in Milne Bay, Morobe, Enga, Eastern Highlands and Southern Highlands.

Beach Sands — Interest in iron-ore beach sands is continuing but testing so far has not resolved processing problems.

Limestone — Limestone occurs in the Highlands, Gulf, Morobe, East New Britain, West New Britain, New Ireland, Chimbu, Enga, Southern Highlands and Western Provinces. Lime kilns or cement manufacturing facilities could be established if there is sufficient demand for the end product.

Coal — Thin seams of coal are exposed in the foothills of the Western, Southern Highlands, Gulf, West Sepik and Morobe.

Bauxite — Small deposits of bauxite have been found at various localities but grade and volumes are not economical.

Chromite — A placer deposit on the Morobe Coast, derived from ultrabasic rocks, is being investigated. Similar deposits elsewhere are attracting attention.

Investigatory drilling sites are often in inaccessible places. Helicopters are frequently used to bring in equipment, supplies and personnel.

Petroleum

Oil and gas seeps occur in the Gulf, Western and Southern Highlands Provinces and extend into West Sepik. These seeps indicate the petroleum potential of the Papuan Basin but significant quantities of oil or gas do not necessarily exist below the ground.

There is also petroleum potential in the North New Guinea Basin (onshore in East Sepik, West Sepik and Madang), the Cape Vogel Basin (offshore from Milne Bay), and the New Ireland Basin (offshore northeast of New Ireland and southwest of North Solomons). Drilling has been done but without much success.

The most important petroleum discovery has been the Pasca gas and gas-condensate field in the Papuan Gulf, 260 kilometres west-north-west of Port Moresby. Reserves have been estimated at around 28 billion cubic metres of gas and 24 000 kilolitres of natural gas liquid.

Nearer the coast is the Urama gas discovery, 35 km south-west of Baimuru in the Gulf Province. Reserves have been estimated at around 5.7 billion cubic metres of gas and 95 000 kilolitres of natural gas liquid. Onshore there have been four gas discoveries and one oil and gas discovery.

Petroleum exploration in the Papuan Basin has been going on at a moderately high level. Fourteen wells have been drilled and another one was expected to be drilled late in 1979 or early in 1980.

The following chart shows the locations of existing and potential minerals and petroleum resources.

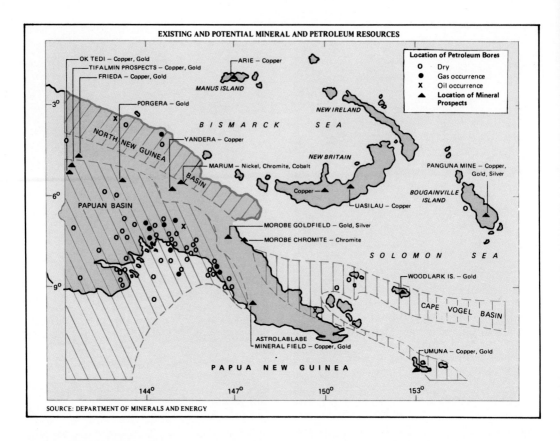

EXISTING AND POTENTIAL MINERAL AND PETROLEUM RESOURCES

Location of Petroleum Bores
O   Dry
●   Gas occurrence
X   Oil occurrence
▲   Location of Mineral Prospects

OK TEDI – Copper, Gold
TIFALMIN PROSPECTS – Copper, Gold
FRIEDA – Copper, Gold
ARIE – Copper
MANUS ISLAND
PORGERA – Gold
NEW IRELAND
NORTH NEW GUINEA
BISMARCK SEA
YANDERA – Copper
BASIN
NEW BRITAIN
PANGUNA MINE – Copper, Gold, Silver
MARUM – Nickel, Chromite, Cobalt
PAPUAN BASIN
Copper
BOUGAINVILLE ISLAND
UASILAU – Copper
MOROBE GOLDFIELD – Gold, Silver
MOROBE CHROMITE – Chromite
SOLOMON SEA
WOODLARK IS. – Gold
CAPE VOGEL BASIN
ASTROLABLABE MINERAL FIELD – Copper, Gold
UMUNA – Copper, Gold
PAPUA NEW GUINEA

144° 147° 150° 153°

SOURCE: DEPARTMENT OF MINERALS AND ENERGY

Mineral and Petroleum Policy

The Government considers the development of mining and petroleum projects should have the highest priority and welcomes foreign investors in undertaking exploration. It has adopted the following basic principles as to the exploitation of mineral and petroleum resources:

- Mineral resources belong to the people of Papua New Guinea. The Government and the people must receive a fair price in return for extraction of the minerals.
- Foreign enterprises exploiting the country's mineral resources deserve a reasonable return on their investments. Extraordinary gains above a reasonable return on investment will go largely to the Government.
- The Government has the right to regulate extractive enterprises. The reasons for this are to maximise the benefits to the local community while minimising the potentially-harmful social and economic effects.

Regulation and control of the exploration and production of minerals and petroleum is one of the the major responsibilities of the Government's Department of Minerals and Energy. This function include allocating prospecting authorities and exploration licences, ensuring legislative obligations are carried out and inspecting such operations to maintain proper safety conditions.

Prospecting concessions are granted by the Minister for Minerals and Energy, who is advised by the Mining Advisory Board and the Petroleum Advisory Board. Areas available for prospecting concessions may be advertised overseas.

The Government's policy regarding petroleum resources covers four objectives, namely:

1. To ensure the maximum financial benefit for Papua New Guinea consistent with allowing a reasonable return to the foreign company;
2. To provide for direct participation by the Government in oil and gas operations;
3. To ensure effective control over the industry through proper financial and technical regulation; and
4. To provide for access by the Government to part of any oil production.

Geologists and their assistants painstakingly record the sub-strata by examining diamond drill cores of the rock below investigation sites.

Exploration

As a general rule, foreign investors will not be allowed to establish small-scale alluvial gold-mining enterprises.

For large-scale exploration, prospecting authorities may be granted for up to two years. Renewal of authorities is dependent on satisfactory completion of agreed work programmes or expenditure of money on prospecting activities and satisfactory proposals for additional work.

For mining purposes, a gold mining lease (maximum area is 20 hectares) or mineral lease (maximum area is 100 ha.) may be granted, both for an initial term not exceeding 21 years. A special mining lease (maximum is 60 square kilometres) may be granted for an initial term not exceeding 42 years, in respect of a very large deposit.

When the existence of a very large deposit is demonstrated, the Government is prepared to enter into firm commitments to ensure the satisfactory establishment of a mine. This is by way of mining agreement with the investor covering the arrangements for each project and providing for the issue of a special mining lease.

As a point of policy, petroleum exploration and production will be undertaken in the private sector. Revenue to the Government will be derived largely from income tax and an additional profit tax charged on cash flows after certain threshold returns have been achieved. The Government will seek a joint interest for its negotiated share of oil produced.

Petroleum prospecting licences, for onshore or offshore areas, may be granted under the Petroleum Act of 1977 for an initial period of six years. An extension period of five years may be granted, dependent on satisfactory completion of agreed work programmes and satisfactory proposals for further work and over not more than 50 per cent of the area.

A petroleum agreement will be negotiated between the Government and the licencee setting out details of how a project should proceed in case of a commercial discovery. Relations between the Government and the licencee will be governed by the petroleum agreement. The licencee, of course, will be subject to the normal laws of Papua New Guinea including the specific laws on petroleum taxation and licensing.

A petroleum agreement provides for the Government's equity participation in future development. It includes provisions on training and localisation, local purchasing and business development, use of facilities by third parties, currency and exchange control, and disposal of the Government's production share.

Energy Development

The Government has adopted a National Energy Policy aimed at self-sufficiency through the increased use of renewable energy resources. It is proposed to use forest resources, waste, hydropower and sunlight to replace increasing imports of petroleum products for power generation. It has also been proposed to use alcohol fuel for transport, produced from cassava, sugar cane and wood.

Total foreign exchange used on imported petroleum products has been increasing rapidly. It represents spending of close to K80 million a year. By the early 1980s, energy imports could demand 20 to 25 per cent of total foreign exchange.

Papua New Guinea's renewable energy potential is possibly the richest of any country in Asia and the Pacific. Government efforts to develop this potential have been through hydropower to produce electricity.

However, a wide range of energy sources have been considered especially in two major sectors, industry and transportation. For example, the Department of Minerals and Energy has plans and funding to set up a project to convert wood waste to oil, charcoal and gas for use as industrial fuels.

The project will be located at the South Pacific timber mill at Lae in the Morobe Province. It will exemplify the wide-ranging social, economic and environmental benefits of an alternative strategy.

Projections show that these energy products will be cheaper significantly than imported petroleum. Furthermore, the energy production facility will reduce considerably the present pollution caused by burning wood wastes close to residential areas. It will also improve the overall economic performance of the forestry industry.

The second major sector which is totally dependent upon imported fuels at present is transportation. It is proposed that a fuel industry be developed to produce power alcohol from sago, cassava and sugarcane. The industry will develop in rural areas first because of the high price of petrol and diesel brought in from coastal ports, thus contributing significantly to economic production in rural areas.

As of early 1979, the Government was paying subsidies of up to K3.50 a gallon to get petrol or diesel to remote communities. The 1977-78 subsidy totalled about K1.7 million and was expected to reach K3 million in 1980.

The Government is also acutely aware of the total dependence of most of the population on firewood for cooking and heating. Although Papua New Guinea has large areas of forests, there are many locations where firewood is in very short supply. For this reason, the Department of Minerals and Energy has undertaken to sponsor projects in growing and harvesting trees for firewood, especially in highly-populated urban settlements and in the Highlands.

Labour and Employment

Workforce

It is difficult to assess the Papua New Guinea workforce accurately in the same context as industrialised nations. Over ninety per cent of the population live in rural areas and practice a subsistence economy. In such an economy people start working at an early age in the food gardens and learning traditional skills. They may continue to work long after the average worker in a more developed society would be considered to have "retired".

Statistics available are based on information from the 1971 Population Census, the Department of Labour and the Public Services Commission. Little accurate information on the rural subsistence labour force is available as a full survey for statistical purposes has not yet been achieved. The National Population Census to be held late in 1980 will shed more light on this question.

The Bureau of Statistics groups available data under a heading of "Population, ten years of age and over, by workforce status and activity". This grouping is divided into those in the money-raising workforce and those not in the money-raising workforce. The latter category includes subsistence workers and those engaged in home duties.

Excluding expatriates, the total workforce has been estimated at 1.25 million. From a base of 1.09 million in 1971 it increased to 1.2 million in 1976 and is expected to increase further to 1.4 million in 1981. (See Table 1).

About 85 per cent are non-wage earners. That is they fall into a category that includes those engaged in farming, fishing, small-scale manufacturing, and the provision of transport and trading services. The remaining 15 per

Plantation labourers 'lain' (line-up) to have their picking weighed, recorded and paid for.

cent are employees working for wages or salaries. Table 2 shows the estimated distribution by activity from 1973-1978.

There is a wide variation in the standard of education in the workforce. Reference to the section on Education will show that relatively few of those that start primary school complete secondary studies to a level where they can be admitted for trade or tertiary training. There is already a surplus of school leavers from high schools over the number of places that are available for training as well as wage or salaried job opportunities. Despite government efforts to provide training facilities there is a shortage of skilled people including manageral personnel as well as a surplus of educated unskilled labour.

There is a great demand for personnal at enpervisory and executive levels. As a result there is an increasing turnover of qualified staff through employers outbidding one another for scarce qualified people. Many organisations provide on-the-job training and also send their more proving employees overseas to widen their experience and upgrade their technical skills.

There is a large potential pool of labour if job opportunities were available. The government works with the private sector to provide individually planned training programmes to meet the needs of industries and services.

Table 1

ESTIMATES OF INDIGENOUS LABOUR FORCE
(aged 10 years or more)
(figures in thousand)

Area and Sex	1971	1976	1981
Rural Village			
Males	508.3	512.3	522.0
Females	838.2	405.6	434.7
Persons	891.5	917.9	956.7
Rural Non-Village			
Males	86.7	121.8	159.4
Females	15.5	24.2	34.0
Persons	102.2	148.0	193.4
Urban			
Males	79.7	122.1	173.9
Females	14.1	23.6	35.5
Persons	93.8	145.7	209.4
TOTAL			
Males	674.7	756.2	855.3
Females	412.8	453.4	504.2
Persons	1 087.5	1 209.6	1 359.5

Note: The above estimates refer to total labour force and not only the market labour force.

SOURCE: DEPARTMENT OF LABOUR AND INDUSTRY

Table 2

WAGE AND SALARY EMPLOYMENT OF NATIONALS

Economic Activity	1973	1975	1977	1978
Plantation agriculture	47 301	41 219	35 563	36 963
Plantation cattle	1 140	980	1 092	1 044
Pig, poultry, milk	830	730	815	787
Other crops	190	289	421	399
Fishing	558	666	606	651
Forestry	3 157	2 157	2 414	2 843
Mining	4 576	3 148	3 508	3 607
Sawmills and joineries	4 186	3 265	4 754	5 445
Engineering, metal and electrical work	1 433	949	1 199	1 158
Vehicle, ships & aircraft repairs	1 632	2 153	2 581	2 557
Beverages	1 066	1 202	1 554	1 455
Tobacco & cigarettes	687	520	728	680
Crop processing and other manufacturing	2 474	1 752	1 799	1 788
Other manufacturing	2 655	2 365	2 985	3 052
Electricity	918	1 697	1 975	1 932
Building and Construction	12 463	11 032	15 442	14 646
Transport	10 715	7 576	9 756	9 685
Communication	1 058	1 826	2 164	2 122
Commerce	10 533	6 610	8 038	7 862
Property investment and financial institutions	1 185	2 324	2 650	2 610
Education	17 434	24 189	25 272	25 171
Health	5 330	7 774	8 113	8 037
Government welfare and religious services	26 041	40 213	43 319	43 035
Other community and business services	1 027	769	881	871
Amusement and personal services	14 750	13 719	16 571	15 900
TOTAL	173 339	179 124	194 200	194 300

SOURCE: THE NATIONAL PUBLIC EXPENDITURE PLAN 1978-1981
        NATIONAL PLANNING OFFICE

Expatriate employment

The government realises the need for expatriate technical staff to establish and maintain some operations. Training of national staff is emphasised in their conditions of employment.

In particular there are certain areas of foreign investments that can not be effectively operated in the early stages without expatriate expertise to handle the administrative and technical problems that arise.

Work permits are granted to foreign experts who can genuinely contribute to the development of the country provided there are no Papua New Guinea nationals available with the necessary qualifications to undertake the work.

The employment of expatriates in Papua New Guinea is controlled and regulated by the Employment of Non-Citizens Act of 1978. Employers may not employ an overseas person in a work category that has been declared prohibited. Employment of foreigners in restricted categories is subject to conditions and is for a limited duration.

There are about 350 categories of occupations that are either prohibited to expatriates or restricted, with provisions for exemptions in special circumstances. Copies of the list may be obtained from the Employment Regulation Section of the Department of Labour and Industry.

Localisation

Table 3 shows the degree of localisation in 500 randomly selected companies in the private sector. In the public service, approximately 90 per cent of positions are now held by nationals. Therefore both the Government and the price sector will have to continue employing qualified expatriates for priority areas during the next few years.

However, steps have been taken to lessen reliance on overseas personnel with the two-fold aim of producing more employment opportunities for Papua New Guineans and reducing labour costs. Private employers hiring expatriate staff are required to introduce effective training and localisation programme that will satisfy the Government. In most cases, the employer must provide a national counterpart to the expatriate worker so that the national can take over after a period of specialist training.

Table 3

PERCENTAGE OF PAPUA NEW GUINEANS IN 500 COMPANIES
(Randomly Selected By Occupation)

Occupation	Percentage
Executive, managerial	17
Professional, technical	30
Managerial (farm and plantations)	40
Clerical	74
Sales	90
Miscellaneous	90
Semi-skilled	92
Farm and plantation workers	100
AVERAGE TOTAL	87

SOURCE: DEPARTMENT OF LABOUR AND INDUSTRY

Employment Conditions.

All workers in Papua New Guinea enjoy certain rights and protection under the country's labour laws. Their health, safety, welfare and basic conditions of employment are guaranteed by national law and regulations administered by the Department of Labour and Industry.

Among the principal functions of the Department of Labour and Industry is the encouragement of liaison and negotiation between employees, employers and the Govern-

ment on all aspects of labour relations; the administration of legislation on employment; the provision of employment placement, and assistance to management; industrial safety and conditions and workers' compensation; control of registration of industrial organisations; general research on labour policy and industrial statistics; and administration of legislation on Weights and Measures.

The employment of workers is regulated by the Employment Act of 1978. The Act provides for working hour limitations, rest periods, paid public holidays, sick and recreation leave, payment of wages, compensation for employment injury or death, dismissal indemnity and standards for the employment of women and children.

In urban areas, a 42-hour week is the minimum standard. The working time commonly observed is eight hours from Monday to Friday and two hours between 7 a.m. and 12 noon on Saturday. Time worked in excess of eight hours in any one day is overtime and a total of 12 hours (including overtime) per day is the maximum permitted. Minimum overtime penalty rates are time and one half, Monday to Saturday, and double time on Sundays and public holidays. Time off is allowed in lieu of payment for the overtime worked and an employee cannot be given less than four hours' work or equivalent pay on a Sunday or public holiday. Salaries are usually paid on a forthnightly basis.

Employees in urban areas are entitled to three weeks paid annual leave after completion of 12 months continuous service. There are eight paid legal annual public holidays and any public holidays occurring during the period of leave are additional to the leave entitlement. Sick leave entitlements are nine days paid sick leave per year and sick leave credits can accumulate to a maximum of 27 days.

Wages

Working conditions are oversighted by the Government and minimum wages are periodically reviewed under a system of minimum wage determinations provided under the Industrial Relations Act and Regulations. Actual wage levels for skilled workers are considerably higher than the minimum set rates and are determined by collective bargaining. In other words, marker rates prevail.

The Minimum Wages Board Determination No. 1 of 1977 has been the instrument of wage adjustments generally since 1977 and shall continue to be the case until it ceases to have effect on 1st March 1980. Generally, employers both public and private have adopted and followed the Board's formula of wage adjustment for workers on superior wage levels.

As at 1st March 1979, the minimum urban wage rose to K30.82 per week. A two-level rural minimum wage system has been in existence since 1974 and currently the minimum wage for the lowest paid workers in "Primary Industries" is K11.45 while the rate for workers in "Other Rural Industries" is K11.93.

In addition to the basic wage level, employers are liable for the insurance of all workers under the provisions of the Worker's Compensation Act of 1978. Legislation provides a single compensation code for workers, with a stepped-up scale of compensation in accordance with wages.

Training and Education

The temporary admission ot foreign workers is currently allowed if they are deemed essential to the development of Papua New Guinea. The Government must be satisfied that there are no Papua New Guineans available with the skills prescribed in occupations to be filled by non-citizens, in which case a suitable training programme is required.

Except for some trades, almost all formalised training of skilled tradesmen is carried out through the apprenticeship training programme. The main part of the apprenticeship training is practical and is provided on the job by the employer. The other part of training is theoretical, done mostly at technical colleges except for some employers which have their own training centres.

The Apprenticeship Board of Papua New Guinea administers the apprenticeship scheme wherein youths who complete their apprenticeships and pass their final examinations are granted trade certificates.

Education requirements vary for entry into the various categories of apprenticeship training and minimum wage rates for apprentices are set under the system. Most apprenticeship is by a block-release system under which apprentices attend a technical school on a residential basis for about five weeks in the year and are then required, in their own time, to take correspondence lessons or attend classes, in addition to their on-the-job training. Apprenticeships are available in about 58 trades, the majority of which require a four-year apprenticeship.

Generally, the minimum education standard required for entry into some engineering and mechanical trades is a satisfactory pass at School Certificate Level (4th year at secondary school). Four year apprenticeships require a satisfactory pass at Form III level (three year) and three-year apprenticeships require a satisfactory pass at Form II level. All apprenticeship wages are related to the wages paid to tradesmen and range from 35 per cent in the first year to 85 per cent in the 4th year of training.

Industrial Organisations

It is Government policy to encourage and assist in the formation and development of stable industrial organisations both for employee and employer groups. An Employer's Federation of Papua New Guinea is registered as an industrial organisation to promote the interests of employers, especially their representation in labour management matters.

Many employee groups that cover either specific industries or workers on a regional basis are registered and are encouraged to increasingly engage in the educational, social and cultural welfare of members in addition to their traditional trade union functions. The system of industrial relations in operation in Papua New Guinea has proved to be very successful in protecting the legitimate rights of employers and workers and in maintaining industrial peace.

Business Development

Traditional trading

In the "time before" there was much contact with foreign traders and for a considerable period of the early colonisation days. Papua New Guineans were self-sufficient in their basic needs. Subsistence farming and gathering from the natural environment was sufficient to supply most of their wants except for exotic articles used for personal adornment or traditional ceremonies.

These and the few other goods they needed were exchanged with groups near and far by a system of barter using goods or 'shell money' as the medium for trade.

Extensive trading networks like the Motuan Hiri voyages or the Kula of the Milne Bay Province islands, not only ensured the supply of the few articles that were needed but kept tribal groups in contact with each other on a regular basis at a social and cultural level.

The colonisers took over, or bartered with clan groups, for large tracts of land and set up plantations using the local people as labour. Foreign traders established trading posts for passing ships, plantations, missions and the few expatriates who administered the colonies. In turn they exported the products of the plantations and the much sought after natural products of the land like Bird of Paradise and crocodile skins.

Traditional shell money or the State's official currency all have their place in the economy.

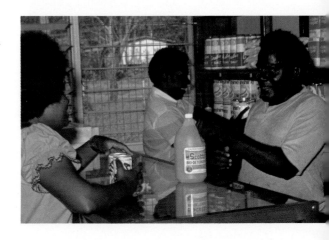

Traditional sailing 'lagatois' of the Hiri trading voyage contrast sharply with the white man's sailing ship (Historical photo taken in Port Moresby harbour at the turn of the century).

Whilst Papua New Guineans of that time were astute businessmen in trading through their traditional circuits they had little to do with the wider world of business and commerce that was extracting great wealth from the land.

Australia, as the last coloniser, and later the first Papua New Guinea Government, inherited an economy dominated by foreigners and foreign interests. Despite Australian Government efforts to introduce foreign business principles and practice Independence overtook the progress towards vesting business interests in local hands.

The Somare Government approached independence with this economic millstone around its neck and was determined to do something about it.

A major point of the Eight Point Plan is to increase the proportion of the economy controlled by Papua New Guineans and the National Development Strategy is geared to achieving this aim.

The National Government has established a number of departments and statutory bodies to oversight the nation's economic activity. Determined measures are being taken to promote local participation in business and commerce and gradually by regulating the amount of expatriate participation in the economy it is slowly passing to Papua New Guinean control.

The Department of Commerce is responsible for formulating overall business development policy on a national scale. These responsibilities include:

- Examining and drafting business legislation.
- Providing advice for large national projects.
- Carrying out research into new business opportunities.
- Managing national training institutions and their programmes.

Some development functions have been decentralised to Provincial Governments which are responsible for:

- Maintaining contact with government departments and private bodies to promote provincial plans for business development.
- Spreading awareness of business opportunities and assisting with their organisation.
- Conducting training courses in business management.
- Advising people wishing to go into business.
- Acting as provincial representatives of the Department of Commerce, the Papua New Guinea Development Bank and the National Investment and Development Authority.

Investment

The people of Papua New Guinea, at the present time, lack both the funds and the management skills to make an appreciable contribution to the private sector. For the foreseeable future, therefore, the private sector in the country will be dependent on foreign investment, and imported management skills.

The Government has set priorities on activities where foreign investment is most needed, and is actively promoting foreign investment into those activities. The Government encourages long-term foreign investment which will give substantial returns to the investor over a period of time. It certainly does not encourage short-term, quick-return investment from overseas.

Foreign Investment – Promotion and Regulation

Foreign investment is an essential part of the National Development Strategy. With this in mind and to ensure planned investment, the Government has set up a statutory body to promote, regulate and control foreign enterprises.

In 1974 Parliament passed the National Investment and Development Act. The Act provides for the promotion of investment (particularly foreign investment) and its regulation and control in the interests of national development. The Act established the National Investment and Development Authority known generally as NIDA.

The Act requires NIDA to prepare a National Investment Priorities Schedule at least once a year. This document is divided into three parts: Priority Activities, Open Activities and Reserved Activities.

Through this schedule foreign investment is guided into those areas where it is most needed. These areas not only give a reasonable return to the investor but give the greatest economic benefit to the nation.

Priority and Open Activities

Foreign investment in Priority Activities is considered essential for Papua New Guinea's development programmes over the coming years. These activities are in resource development: minerals and petroleum, agriculture, forestry, and fishing and all large-scale and capital intensive projects requiring high technology.

In minerals, considerable exploratory work has been done. At least one mining project is expected to come in to operation in the next few years. The Bougainville Copper Project was in existence prior to the establishment of NIDA and the agreement for its operation was re-negotiated by the Government as a special case.

Foreign investment has been responsible for the Bougainville Copper Mine . . .

In petroleum, exploratory drilling has been under way for many years. Commercial finds have yet to be established.

It is in agriculture that Papua New Guinea has been most successful in attracting foreign investment. Three large nucleus-estate oil palm schemes have been established. Each scheme being about 10 000 hectares in size. A fourth scheme is currently being negotiated. The investment in a project of this nature is in the range of K20 million to K30 million.

. . . and the West New Britain oil palm industry.

A sugar scheme which will provide about 30 000 to 40 000 tonnes of sugar per annum, (the country's estimated annual consumption by 1982) is being negotiated. This project alone may have a total capitalisation of about K65 million, most of which will comprise overseas funds.

A wide variety of primary products are being investigated, improved, processed or produced with the help of foreign capital.

The country's first commercial rice project: a large-scale, irrigated, mechanised scheme on about 20 000 hectares was expected to start late in 1979. The project will supply about 15 000 tonnes of rice. This is only a fraction of the country's consumption which runs to about 80 000 tonnes per year. There is scope for four or five such schemes.

Negotiations are being held to start the first nucleus-estate rubber scheme on about 3 000 hectares.

NIDA has been seeking foreign investment to open up large-scale, nucleus-estate cocoa plantations.

In timber, foreign investment has been slow. This is mainly because of the depressed state of the international timber industry in recent years. However, there have been negotiations for a timber project involving some 5.8 million cubic metres of logs, and about 7.3 million cubic metres of pulpwood. Opportunities are still available for investment in timber exploitation in many other areas throughout the country.

In fishing, Government policy has been to allow foreign fishing fleets to harvest the fishing resources in the short term, till such time as the country has its own fishing fleets. In the long term, in tuna fishing, a sustainable catch of

Skipjack tuna fishing from Papua New Guinea's waters has a potential harvest second only to those of Japan and the United States of America.

100 000 tonnes per annum is feasible. Even with harvesting being done by foreign fleets, NIDA wishes to see the catch landed on Papua New Guinea shores.

Negotiations are in advanced stage for the establishment of a tuna fish processing plant in Kavieng.

Opportunities are available also for foreign investment in the prawn and lobster-fishing industry.

In almost all these large-scale projects the Government takes up a substantial equity investment.

Open and Reserved Activities

The second category in the Priorities Schedule is the Open Activities category, an area in which foreign investment is not as actively sought. However, foreign investment is allowed in this category, depending on individual merit.

The third category in the Priorities Schedule is the Reserved Activites category. These are activities in which, as a general rule, foreign investment is not allowed. These are activities which either do not require high technology or are not capital-intensive. They are therefore more suited to national entrepreneurs.

Incentives

An incentive to foreign investment in Papua New Guinea is the country's political stability.

In certain circumstances, where the private sector has not taken the initiative, the Government has been packaging projects. On many of these the Government has formed the company, subscribed initial capital, identified foreign investors, appointed project managers, and finally, phased itself out of active management leaving the project under private sector management. The Government retains representation on the company's board if there is substantial Government equity in the project.

Papua New Guinea's Development Strategy has two important investment aspects: the Government acting as a catalyst in setting up private companies; and the Government's non-interference once such companies have been set up. The setting up of state-owned corporations has been avoided, a common practice in many developing countries which has led to disaster in a number of instances.

The Government does not offer tax holidays and similar incentives to investors. However it may meet part of the costs of any feasibility studies for setting up an industry in Papua New Guinea, capitalising such expenses in the form of shares in the company if the project is carried out.

As an incentive to companies in the manufacturing industries to export their products, profits related to any increase in exports in any year are allowed a tax rebate of 50 per cent.

The infant-industry loan assistance scheme provides for loan assistance from the Government to companies in their initial stages.

There has been a slight increase in corporate taxes which has brought the corporate tax for resident companies to 36.5 per cent. This is still appreciably lower than that prevailing in most other countries. In addition, there is a 15 per cent dividend withholding tax on dividends declared and paid to overseas shareholders.

The Government guarantees foreign investment the free flow of funds to meet dividend payments, overseas loan interest and debt servicing. It also guarantees there will be no expropriation except on the payment of full compensation.

The Government's success in attracting foreign investment is indicated by the fact that between the beginning of January 1975 and the end of 1978, some 957 new foreign enterprises have been registered with NIDA. Within this period, some 8 000 new jobs were created and a foreign capital investment of K136 million generated.

In view of the large number of major projects that have been negotiated, the level of foreign investment is expected to show a marked rise in the future.

Local capital investment

As well as the major development projects, financed largely by foreign capital, many opportunities exist for the business minded citizen to enter commerce as an entrepreneur or as an investor.

The Investment Corporation of Papua New Guinea was established in 1971 to take up equity in business enterprises for the benefit of Papua New Guineans. The Corporation has set up a fund within its organisation called the Investment Corporation Fund which is wholly owned by Fund shareholders. As citizens subscribe money to the Fund, the Investment Corporation transfers selected equities to it. The dividends earned by these transferred equities are available for distribution to shareholders.

In this way Papua New Guineans with only limited savings are able to invest them in companies that are virtually 'safe'. Money that would otherwise be lying idle can thus be used for national development.

Other investment possibilities are available through the Papua New Guinea Banking Corporation and the other banks in the type of securities that trading and savings banks normally offer.

Savings and Loans Societies have been started, generally in connection with business organisations. Savings are made by regular deductions from income and small loans for specific purposes can be obtained.

Business Assistance

The Department of Commerce will assist the implementation of business proposals which are likely to succeed and become self-reliant projects. Projects that will benefit rural areas and a large number of people are preferred.

Among the business projects given considerable assistance during the past few years were those involving land transportation, small industries, vegetable marketing, building contracts, plantation take-over, and expansion of wholesale and retail activities. In the small industries category, two examples may serve to illustrate how assistance from the Department has helped to establish industries particularly suitable for the rural sector.

Subsistence farming on a mountainside in the densely populated Chimbu Province.

Sericulture — There are over 400 smallholder farmer projects in the Southern and Western Highlands. Extension staff of the Department are posted to a number of locations to service and supervise the smallholders in these areas. Silkworm eggs have been imported regularly and cocoons exported, producing a self-generating income for the people.

Handcrafts — The Department's Handcrafts Section acts as a buy-and-sell facility for handcrafts. Regular buying trips have been carried out to major craft-producing areas. This service seeks to ensure that rural producers have a regular outlet for their products and national dealers have a regular supply of handcrafts.

Development Funds Availability

For those with expertise but limited capital who wish to set up their own business, loan funds are available through a number of agencies. It has already been explained that one of the functions of the Department of Commerce is to assist citizens into business enterprises if their projects are viable and they have the expertise to promote them.

The Papua New Guinea Development Bank has been expressly set up to assist this process by granting loans to individuals and groups on a very favourable interest and repayment programme. Loans from the Bank are generally in excess of K500 and they require a substantial amount of the total funds requirement (normally half) to be found by the individual or group seeking the loan. The Bank will investigate the project to satisfy itself that it is viable and that the loan can be repaid in a reasonable time from the project's expected income.

Commercial Banks also make loan money available but generally their terms are more strict than those of the Development Bank.

The Village Economic Development Fund (VEDF), administered by the Department of Commerce, makes funds available for businesses in rural areas. Grants covering up to 40 per cent of a project's initial cost may be given. The balance is normally provided by a loan from the Development Bank plus any money the group seeking assistance has. Preference for VEDF assistance is given to groups in remote areas with little opportunity for earning a cash income. Groups often make their contributions in the form of cash, material or labour.

Some activities assisted by VEDF are: artifact production and distribution, agricultural

projects, bakeries, building contracts, crocodile farming, logging and sawmilling, retail trading, road maintenance contracts, transport and tourist facilities.

Birds of Paradise are strictly protected and may be taken for traditional use only.

The crocodile, however, is being farmed by villagers, for sale on export markets.

In 1975 the Government introduced the Plantation Acquisition Scheme under which expatriate owned plantations whose owners wished to sell, received a 'fair' price from the Government for their properties. The Government then sells the plantation to the local people for their joint management. Many groups have used the facilities described above to 'buy back' land that has been developed by expatriates for many years.

Trade stores have also passed to Papua New Guinean management in the same way. A number of these have been oversighted by Development Bank officers and a chain known as Stret Pasin Stoas has been established. The scheme provides finance for buying supplies, training of prospective owners and providing employment for a period before the opportunity to buy is offerred to the manager operating each store.

Research and Development

The Department of Commerce's Small Industries Research and Development Centre has workshops in metalworking, woodworking, pottery, leatherwork and rubber-moulded goods. Research is carried out into the technical feasibility of potential small industries. If the viability of an activity is fully proven, a pilot-project is started before being passed on to a suitable private entrepreneur.

The Department of Commerce helps many tradesmen into small scale businesses of their own.

Numerous groups have sought the Department's assistance for the registration of their businesses. In addition, locally-owned companies have obtained benefits under the Co-operative Companies Act of 1975.

The Department also promotes women's participation in business. It has been giving advice and other assistance to businesswomen in such undertakings as coffee bars and food shops.

Bank agencies are located throughout the country.

Training

The Department of Commerce conducts training courses at the Laloki College at Laloki near Port Moresby, and field training in other centres.

The College trains officers of the Department in skills necessary to enable them to function effectively as business advisors. It also trains private businessmen and their employees in management and general business skills in retail and wholesale trading, transport, building contracting and primary-produce marketing.

The College offers a Certificate of Business Management Course which is relevant to a Business Development Officer's work.

A Field Training Section in the Department has been in operation since 1973. Courses are offered to businessmen in the provinces on various subjects. Among these are courses on trade stores, short-produce marketing, public motor vehicle (PMV) and land transport operation, book-keeping, and business principles.

The Department also offers a Plantation Management Training Programme (PMTP) which is based at Rabaul in East New Britain. The programme trains plantation managers and directors as well as cocoa-fermenting operators in cocoa processing. PMTP acts as an agricultural management training resource for other Government departments and organisations.

Private Sector Co-operation

Businessmen and business enterprises have co-operated with the Government in promoting business development. Many of them belong to chambers of commerce of which there are about 10 based in the major centres.

In turn, these chambers have grouped themselves into one organisation called the Associated Chambers of Commerce. The organisation has been helping to develop both domestic and foreign trade. It has been involved in the formulation of the national investment policy and negotiations with foreign businessmen and establishments.

In keeping with the Government's localisation programme, the Associated Chambers of Commerce members have been employing an increasing number of nationals and training them for more responsible positions. Major business enterprises employ an average of about 90 per cent Papua New Guineans.

Communications:

Traditional transport between coastal villages was by sailing canoe. Canoes are still extensively used and everything needed for long voyages is provided – including the cooking fire.

Transport

Over the years transport has played a vital role in the history of Papua New Guinea's development.

Exploration and development in the country is synonymous with the growth of the transport infrastructure and services. Sea, land and air transport each has influenced the pattern of economic growth.

The mainland coast and many islands have been explored and their resources developed by means of water transport. The copra industry, which supplies a major part of the country's export earnings, has been depending considerably on sea transport. Coconut plantations have been located generally near small ship anchorages.

In the Gazelle Peninsula and on the Madang coast, copra has been moved from the plantations to the small ports for shipment by road. In the Papuan region, pack animals were used to serve the rubber estates of the Sogeri plateau and the missions in the Goilala hill country.

Air transport has been essential in providing access to the hinterland. With the discovery of gold in the Wau-Bulolo area in the 1920s, Papua New Guinea led the world in pioneering freight movement by air. From the close of World War II, the development of the Highlands region was carried out almost entirely by air transport.

Papua New Guinea gives considerable importance to the improvement of its sea, land and air transport. Its transport policy emphasises the development of a reliable transport system that will link rural areas to nearby towns and population centres to regional ports.

Small coastal trading vessels meet up with the big international freighters at the main ports to tranship cargo for overseas markets.

The agency responsible for setting out the Government's transport policy and programmes is the Department of Transport and Civil Aviation. Transport services are supplied mainly by private companies, with limited control by the Government.

Marine Transport

Shipping is the oldest and most important form of social and economic communication for the coastal and island people. This is illustrated by the continued celebration of the "Hiri Moale" in the Central Province and the "Kula" trade in the Milne Bay area.

Over the years, shipping has not lost its central role in the life of the nation. On the contrary, the need for shipping has become greater.

The type of shipping needed has changed, however, from the traditional canoe to the workboat and more recently to the large, modern-cargo vessel. These changes have come about because of the need to transport larger volumes and units of cargo.

Regulation. Shipping is regulated by means of the Merchant Shipping Act of 1975. This law is enforced by the Division of Marine of the Department of Transport and Civil Aviation. The Division has four main objectives:

- Improved safety of all ships;
- Improved shipping services throughout the country;
- Extending Papua New Guinea's involvement in overseas shipping and trade; and
- Training Papua New Guineans to administer and operate the shipping industry.

The Division's safety function includes: administering the surveys of vessels and safety equipment; advising the shipping industry and other Government departments regarding compliance with the Merchant Shipping Act and the construction of small boats; and testing new marine products for approval as safety appliances.

Another aspect of the Division's concern for sea safety is its search-and-rescue operations. It responds to emergency situations which arise in or around ports or at sea, such as people being lost overboard as well as vessels running aground, catching fire or experiencing difficulties.

The Division encourages village groups to own and operate their own workboats for transporting primary products and other trade goods to and from central collection points. It has been consulting with the Provincial Governments to determine collection points. It has also been finding out how to improve the production and cut the cost of new workboats.

Shipping demand. The demand for sea transport is increasing rapidly due to rising costs of building and maintaining roads. In terms of maintenance and operating costs, water transport is the cheapest form of transport.

The national shipping line, Papua New Guinea Shipping Corporation, was founded in 1977 to lead and set standards in the development of maritime transport services associated with the country's internal and external trade.

In 1978, the PNG Shipping Corporation bought a major shareholding in the leading coastal shipping operator, Mainport Cargoes, and took over the management of the company. Mainport Cargoes has made rapid progress towards establishing scheduled, reliable liner services linking the main ports.

There are about 130 vessels licensed to operate on Papua New Guinea's coastal waters. They provide coastal shipping services between main ports and feeder ports, and carry passengers, general cargo, refrigerated goods and liquid bulk cargo.

Some progress has been made in modernising feeder services to main ports, with several new vessels replacing obsolete ones. Shipping services have also been upgraded to reduce dependence on air transport, especially in coastal and island regions.

Cargo liner services operate between Papua New Guinea and ports in Australia, Europe, Hong Kong, Japan, New Zealand, North and South America, Pacific Islands, and Singapore.

The Papua New Guinea Harbours Board is responsible for the administration, operation and control of movement of ships, and cargo handling within the country's four regional ports and 12 satellite ports. The regional ports are Port Moresby, Lae, Rabaul and Madang. The satellite ports are Samarai, Oro Bay, Alotau, Daru, Kieta, Kavieng, Kimbe, Buka, Wewak, Aitape, Vanimo and Lorengau.

Considerable expansion of port facilities has been taking place. A port development programme was started in 1973, and about K24 million has been spent on port projects. Latest projects included the upgrading of overseas wharves at Port Moresby and Kieta, and wharf improvements at Alotau and Samarai.

There are 102 lighted navigational aids throughout the country. Another 200 unlighted beacons are maintained by the Division of Marine.

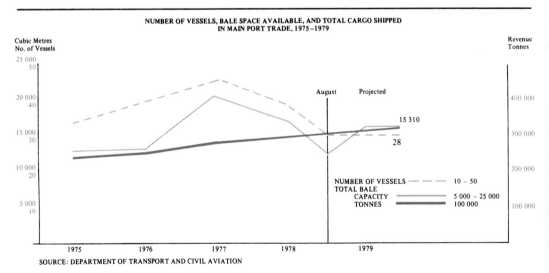

NUMBER OF VESSELS, BALE SPACE AVAILABLE, AND TOTAL CARGO SHIPPED IN MAIN PORT TRADE, 1975–1979

SOURCE: DEPARTMENT OF TRANSPORT AND CIVIL AVIATION

110

In mountain terrain road making can be a hazardous operation. Gigantic landslides can disrupt traffic for days on the Highlands Highway. Sometimes major re-alignment is the only answer to the problem.

Training. The Nautical Training Institute in the Madang Province trains Papua New Guineans for positions in the shipping industry, including trainee pilots for the Harbours Board.

The Institute's training programme concentrates on Coastal Certificates which prepare trainees to man the coastal fleet. It also offers a course leading to the Certificate of Restricted Radiotelephone Operator.

The Institute's facilities include a marine engineering workshop, a seamanship room and a workboat. The marine engineering workshop is used for shore instruction on the maintenance and operation of diesel engines and auxiliary engine-room equipment. Instruction on knots, splices and other skills of a trained seaman is conducted in the seamanship room. The workboat, donated by the New Zealand Government, is used for training in shiphandling, seamanship and operation of radar and radio.

In addition, the Papua New Guinea Shipping Corporation trains Papua New Guineans in various aspects of ship management and operation.

Land Transport

The main emphasis of the Government's land transport development programme is on improving the road network. Roads are vital to the densely-populated provinces in the Highlands and agricultural areas like the North Solomons, New Ireland, East New Britain and East Sepik Provinces.

The road network comprises about 18 350 kilometres of vehicular roads, of which only about three per cent is sealed. Most urban roads are sealed.

The principal roads extend from the major ports of Port Moresby, Lae, Madang, Wewak, Kavieng, Rabaul, Kimbe, Buka and Kieta. These roads connect agricultural areas on populated centres to ports through which import-export trade is handled.

Secondary roads provide access to markets for large populations engaged in growing coffee, tea, tobacco, timber, pyrethrum, cattle and other primary products. Many of these roads are in the Highlands Provinces.

Roads and bridges. Climate and terrain make road construction work in Papua New Guinea

A bulldozer edges an access track along a mountainside or a small army of human labour moves the dirt to cut or fill. Even more roads are demanded by rural villagers and townspeople alike.

'Rush-hour' in Port Moresby and a policeman regulates the traffic at a pedestrian crossing at the bottom of Three Mile hill.

exceedingly difficult and expensive. Almost half of works programme expenditures go to road construction projects. The Government spent some K30 million from 1976 to 1978 for roads and bridges projects.

The 1979-82 National Public Expenditure Plan covers the construction of several roads and bridges, maintenance of existing ones and road sealing. Planned expenditure for these projects amounts to about K62 million for the four-year period. The Highlands Highway project is the major project and includes the sealing of 112 kilometres of road and the construction of 14 bridges.

The drafting and evaluation of proposals for road construction, improvement and maintenance, is one of the main functions of the Land Transport Division of the Department of Transport and Civil Aviation.

Control. The Land Transport Division performs the following other functions:

- Prepare, in conjunction with other Government departments and agencies, legislative proposals on road use;
- Issue, through the Land Transport Board, operative licences for passenger-carrying vehicles operated for hire or reward;
- Issue licences for motor car dealers;
- Control the maximum rates which may be charged by for-hire carriers for passengers and freight;
- Enforce the weight limitations applicable to various classes of vehicles, especially those used to carry freight;
- Implement a road safety programme, in co-operation with the police and other agencies;
- Control the importation of road vehicles and spare parts; and
- Analyse (as required) road transport statistics published by the Bureau of Statistics and, in addition, collect and analyse some other kinds of road data.

Air Transport

Air transport was introduced in Papua New Guinea in the early 1920s, and developed more quickly than it did in some developed countries. For example, in the 1930s, airplanes moved more cargo in Papua New Guinea than was moved in Britain, France, Germany and the United States. Today there are few parts of Papua New Guinea that are not served by aircraft.

Aviation forms a major part of the transport system. In many areas, air services provide the only means of transport to remote inland centres and are an important factor in developing these areas.

Regulation. Under the 1973 Interim Arrangement Act, responsibility for regulating the aviation industry is shared by the Papua New Guinea and Australian Governments. The Australian Government is represented by the Civil Aviation Agency based in Port Moresby.

In regulating air transport, the Civil Aviation Division of the Department of Transport and Civil Aviation carries out the following functions:

- Policy and planning — This includes licensing of civil aviation operators, granting of air routes, approval of timetables for international and domestic operators, import and export of aircraft,

approval of fares and freight rates, recovery from users of the cost of aviation facilities including air navigation charges, negotiation of international air service agreements with other countries, and granting of permits for charter operations and overflights by foreign aircraft;

- Operations — This includes rescue and fire-fighting services, national aviation security to deter hijacking and un-authorised entry into restricted areas, noise control at airports, and administer-ing the Government-sponsored flying training scholarship scheme which provides opportunity for Papua New Guineans to be trained as pilots; and

- Aerodrome development and monitoring — Aerodromes which are open to the public are inspected every three months to ensure that the safety and regularity of aircraft operations into and out of such places are maintained.

The Civil Aviation Agency's functions cover: air traffic control, flight information and communication, flying operations, planning, communication and flight testing of navigation facilities and communication and airways engineering.

Domestic Services. Domestic air transport is regulated by the issue of air service licences and the import of aircraft. Domestic operations

Papua New Guinea was air transport minded long before many larger countries realised the cargo-carrying potential of the aeroplane. Third level airlines fly to and from hundreds of tiny inland airstrips . . .

comprise those of the national airline, Air Niugini, third-level operators, charter flights, aerial work or flying associated with business activities, and private operations or pleasure flying.

Formed in 1973, Air Niugini provides regular services between main centres with Fokker F27 and F28 aircrafts. Third-level operators service numerous small airstrips, connecting with Air Niugini at major centres.

The biggest third-level operator is Talair, originally called Territory Air Lines. It has a fleet of about 60 modern aircraft.

Another third-level operator is Douglas Airways, formerly Aerial Tours. The Christian missions have been active also in aviation, specially the Mission Aviation Fellowship and the Lutheran Aviation Service.

International services. Regulation of international air transport is carried out through negotiations with other countries. Air Niugini operates regular services to Australia, Indonesia, Hawaii, Hong Kong, Japan, the Philippines, Singapore, and the Solomon Islands through favourable arrangements with these countries.

Other international carriers operate into Papua New Guinea on a regular basis. These carriers include Cathay Pacific Airways of Hong Kong, Philippine Airlines, and Qantas Airways of Australia.

Training. Aviation training is conducted at the Civil Aviation Training College near Jacksons Airport in Port Moresby. The College provides two types of training:
- Operational — Training in the operation of control towers and flight service centres; and
- Technical — On-the-job training in radio and electrical fields. Theoretical components of the course are conducted at the University of Technology in Lae.

Air Niugini trains not only stewards and stewardesses but other airline officers including ticketing and traffic clerks, airport counter representatives, load and despatch workers, and cargo staff.

In addition, Douglas Airways operates the first full-time pilot training establishment. It is called the Douglas Flight Training Centre which offers training for the following: private pilot's licence, commercial pilot's licence, flight instructors rating, and first-class instrument rating.

. . . to link up with the national airline, Air Niugini, at major ports. In its short history Air Niugini has expanded from piston engined DC-3s to the giant Boeing 707 and flies several of the international air routes of the Asia-Pacific region.

Post and Telecommunications

Papua New Guinea's progress in communications has been reflected not only in its increasing and improved transport facilities. The country's postal and telecommunications services have also been increased and improved.

The postal and telecommunications development programme of the Government's Department of Public Utilities aims to provide more and better facilities for widespread and rapid communication.

Postal History

Before the introduction of postal facilities towards the end of the 19th century, unstamped letters and other articles were probably carried for a fee by vessels calling at New Guinea ports. In the early 1880s, a vessel called "Elsea" made

voyages every three months between Thursday Island in Australia and Port Moresby.

With the proclamation of the British protectorate over south-eastern New Guinea in 1884, stamps and an organised postal service became necessary. A regular mail service was established by 1886 between Sydney, Australia, and New Guinea by the "S.S. Victory" owned by Burns, Philp & Co. Ltd.

The earliest known use of stamps was in August 1885 when Queensland stamps were used in Port Moresby, cancelled with the letters "NG" in an eight-barred oval. Other early stamps featured the traditional canoe, "lagatoi", and traditional huts, among others.

In 1888, permanent post offices were opened in Port Moresby and Samarai in the Milne Bay Province. In 1942, postal administration was assumed by the Australian Army Postal Service and Australian stamps were used. The arrival of United States forces and later of

The Port Moresby - Alotau microwave system is the first solar-powered microwave system in the Southern hemisphere.

New Zealand forces resulted in the establishment of American Army post offices and New Zealand field post offices.

After World War II, Papua and New Guinea stamps were destroyed. From the date of transfer from military to civilian control on 30 October 1945, Australian stamps were used.

On 30 October 1952, the first distinctive stamp issue was made for the combined Territory, showing phases of territorial life. Subsequent stamp issues before and after Independence featured the progress in the fields of health, sport, electoral reform, education, air services, industry, conservation and welfare as well as the flora, fauna, artifacts and folklore.

Present Postal Facilities

A full range of postal services except house-to-house delivery of mail is provided. Mail is delivered by means of private and free mail bags, post office boxes and counter services.

Thirty-three official post offices are located mostly at provincial centres. Postal services and facilities in rural areas are provided by some 77 agency post offices.

Facilities are available for the registration of letters, packets and parcels within the domestic post service, and of letters and packets through the overseas post service. There is an insurance service for overseas parcels. Postal order facilities are provided at all official post offices.

A mobile post office van provides postal services to some areas of Port Moresby not served by a post office or agency. It visits markets and other places where there are people who need postal facilities. Its services include sale of stamps and acceptance of regular and registered mail.

Foreign mail. Air mail services operate five times a week between Port Moresby and four cities in Australia, Sydney, Melbourne, Canberra and Brisbane. Air mail services also operate three times weekly to New Zealand, Canada, Hong Kong, Singapore, the Philippines, Fiji and the Solomon Islands.

Surface mail is conveyed between Papua New Guinea and Australia about twice a month. Other services between Papua New Guinea and overseas countries operate at approximately monthly intervals.

Local mail. Domestic mail is conveyed by air, sea and road. Air mail services operate daily from Port Moresby to most provincial centres.

Letters carried by air within Papua New Guinea are not charged any special air mail fee. Parcels, packets and other mail matter, are carried by air on air mail rates.

Philately

The Department of Public Utilities has a Philatelic Bureau which handles stamp dealing and postal stationery. The Bureau has collected many trophies for its philatelic displays arranged through its agents around the world.

Papua New Guinea stamps continue to feature traditional themes. New markets for the country's stamps are continually being established and mail order services are available. Papua New Guinea is a worldwide favourite among stamp collectors.

PNG stamps are leaders in design and internationally popular.

Telecommunications

Telecommunication services comprise telephone, telegraph, telex and picturegram services as well as some data services both within Papua New Guinea and overseas. There are also radio outstation services to remote localities and coastal shipping besides a coastal radio service for national and international shipping.

Full automation. Telephone services in all provincial centres are fully automatic. All centres in the country are in instant dialling contact with one another through Subscriber Trunk Dialling.

Papua New Guinea is served by International Subscriber Dialling Service to Australia and manual connection to the rest of the world. A submarine cable, laid between Port Moresby and Cairns in Northern Australia, has further improved telephone services between Papua New Guinea and other countries.

Telex and telegraphic services operate to more than 73 different countries. Domestic telegraphic services are available at hundreds of telegraph stations throughout the country.

Mailgrams and public telex operate at many provincial centres.

All major centres have radio intercommunications. Small centres and outstations have scheduled radio services.

Land based stations and ships at sea maintain communication through two Radphone stations at Port Moresby and Rabaul.

Solar power. Papua New Guinea's telecommunications service is provided by a 960-channel broadband microwave system that covers the whole of Papua New Guinea. The repeater stations for the network will be operated on solar power by 1982.

The Department of Public Utilities established the first solar system to power a repeater station on Mount Nambamati in the Morobe Province in 1976.

The country's first full telecommunications systems to be powered by solar energy – the Port Moresby to Alotau connection – started operating in December 1978. The system serves the people of eastern Papua. It was the first of its kind, powered by the sun, to be operational anywhere in the world.

119

The training of telecommunication operators, technicians and tradesmen is carried out at the Department's two training colleges at Lae and Port Moresby.

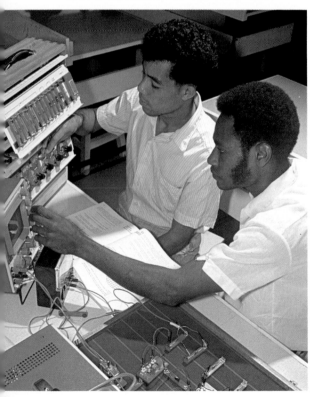

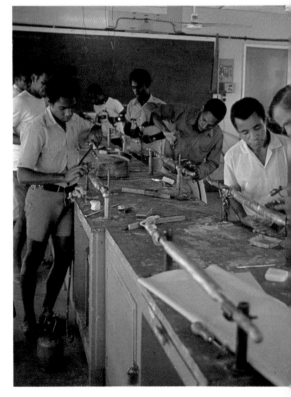

Training

Papua New Guinea gained further headway in postal and telecommunications development with the establishment of the National Postal and Telecommunications Training Centre at Lae in 1978. The Centre caters for technical training requirements of the Department of Public Utilities, particularly radio, telephone, telegraph lines, subscriber equipment and traffic.

In line with the Government's self-reliance policy, the Centre handles its own instructor training, methodology, course development, equipment servicing, and editorial and printing requirements.

The old Post and Telegraphs (P&T) Training College in Port Moresby has become the P & T Non-Technical Training College.

International Affiliations

Papua New Guinea is a member of three international postal organisations: the Commonwealth Conference for Postal Administrations, the Asian-Oceanic Postal Union, and the Universal Postal Union. Membership of these organisations enables the Government to keep abreast of the latest techniques in international mail arrangements and accounts. It has also enabled Papua New Guinea to take advantage of technical assistance programmes provided through these organisations including training scholarships for postal officers.

Papua New Guinea is also a member of the Commonwealth Telecommunications Organisation and the International Telecommunications Union. Through these establishments, the Government keeps abreast of international telecommunications development, including research to improve its telecommunications facilities.

Media

In a nation where over 700 distinct languages are spoken the problems of communication through the media are considerable.

Communications media in Papua New Guinea can be broadly divided into three categories: direct personal contact between persons or groups, radio broadcasting and the print media.

There is no television, although the feasibility of its introduction is being investigated, and the media of film as a home grown product is relatively unexploited.

Direct personal contact with the people is largely the method by which most messages are communicated especially in the area of government.

The larger government departments employ numbers of extension workers. This is particularly so in primary industry, health, education and business development. Their work is backed up with audio-visual aids, broadcast programmes and printed material.

The value of the broadcast medium was recognised at an early stage of the country's development. Virtually the whole population can be reached by radio. The most recent survey estimates that up to 80% do actually listen at some time or other.

Literacy levels are relatively low and most printed material is produced in English, Pidgin or Motu. A few organisations are involved in reducing the spoken word of major language groups to written form. Dictionaries, grammars and a few publications at a primary level are published by these organisations to promote literacy in the first language of these major linguistic groups.

Broadcasting

Radio broadcasting is the principal medium for mass communication. The National Broadcasting Commission has the responsibility of providing a radio broadcasting service to the people. To this end it was constituted by statute in December 1973 at the time Papua New Guinea achieved self-government.

At that time it took over the facilities of the Australian Broadcasting Commission, which had been operating a regional service through Port Moresby and Rabaul, and 15 district radio stations operated by the Administration's Department of Information and Extension Services.

Present transmissions are divided into two services: the National Service from Port Moresby, Lae, Rabaul, Madang, Goroka and and Wewak, and the provincial service transmissions from 19 provincial centres throughout the country.

The National Service is largely broadcast in English. The Provincial services transmit in Pidgin or Motu and a number of languages of the larger linguistic groups in the listening area of each provincial broadcasting station. A total of 19 languages is used and a large proportion of the population can be reached through this medium.

Commercial advertisements are only broadcast on the National Service and only at certain times of the day.

Having representation in all provinces the NBC has the most extensive news reporting system in the country. It also produces programmes that are designed to aid the nation's development strategy. However, a large proportion of programmes fall into the category of entertainment and locally produced music, both of the traditional and modern variety are popular with the listening public.

Imported and local theatre productions complement each other and the works of a number of Papua New Guinean authors and playwrights are produced by the Commission

In conjunction with the Education Department, schools, broadcasts are transmitted daily during school term times. Religious broadcasts, current affairs programmes, discussion groups and sports and other recreation coverage also feature in the broadcasting service.

Print Media

The Papua New Guinea Post Courier (formerly the South Pacific Post) is the oldest newspaper in the country. Presently published five days a week, Monday to Friday it has recently been joined by Niugini Nius which is published four days a week, Tuesday to Friday.

Both of these newspapers are essentially for the English speaking educated section of the community living in urban centres. They are only published in English and whilst some copies may filter down to more remote rural readers their effectiveness as daily newspapers is restricted by the limitations of distribution problems.

A number of less frequently published papers are produced either in English or one or other of the two major lingua franca, Pidgin or Motu.

The largest of these are Wantok (in Pidgin with a weekly frequency) and New Nation (in English with a monthly frequency and primarily intended for young readers). The Government, through the Office of Information, publishes a twice monthly newspaper, Our News, in simple English. It has two lingua franca editions in Pidgin and Motu. These three papers are intended for readers with limited literacy and are widely circulated in the rural areas. They have been published for the last 20 years.

Numerous regional and local news sheets are published by organisations with particular interests but their circulation is generally limited to relatively small areas.

In 1978 the Minister for Media set up a National Newspaper Committee. Its purpose was to look at the feasibility of establishing a national newspaper which would satisfy both the need for a newspaper for rural readership as well as the government's desire to improve communications in these areas.

Since the committee was formed, Niugini Nius has commenced publication, amalgamating three established regional papers, Lae Nius, Ailans Nius and Hailans Nius. However, there is still a gap in the print media for truly rural readership as envisaged by the terms of reference of the National Newspaper Committee.

Despite a low literacy level the demand for printed matter is great. The printing industry is one of the larger secondary industries and all main centres are serviced by one or more printing companies. The biggest concentration of these is in Port Moresby.

As the transportation infrastructure is developed to link remote areas of the country with the towns the demand for published material will be more easily met. The industry generally has a bright future.

The Office of Information

The Office of Information is an office of the Department of the Prime Minister and has responsibility for providing an information service to the people and the National Government.

Its aims are to promote National Government policies and programmes, assess reaction of the people to these and report back to government. It also provides a government news service to media outlets both at home and abroad and produces material for overseas publicity.

Apart from the administrative unit and the Policy Secretariat it is organised around three main divisions. The Information Division services the news media, looks after the public relations function, handles accreditation of foreign journalists and other media representatives and organises publicity displays and exhibitions in overseas countries.

The Government Liaison Division is the extension arm of the Office and constitutes the Office's main contact force with the people.

Amongst its other operations the government's Office of Information provides design, video, photographic and film services.

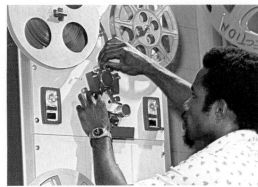

Until the introduction of the decentralisation policy this division had strong representation in every province with a communications network that was capable of reaching the more remote villages.

These offices and networks still exist but their organisation and staffing have been decentralised to provincial governments. They work for the National Government on an agency basis and maintain their links with the former head office in Port Moresby to promote National Government policies.

Project officers in this division work closely with other government departments and agencies and provide expertise for their programmes.

The Production Division is made up of a number of smaller sections each capable of producing specialised material to back up the work of the other divisions of the Office of Information.

The largest of these is the Publications unit which has facilities to design and prepare all types of publications. It has a small offset and silk screen printery to assist in their production.

The Film unit and its sister Video unit are well equipped and have produced many fine films on all aspects of life in Papua New Guinea. They range from short documentaries to full length features. Many have won acclaim and awards in foreign film festivals.

The Photographic unit provides 'still' photographic services to back general publicity, publications and news releases. It also maintains an historical reference library of negatives on the progress of Papua New Guinea's development.

The Design section within the Publications unit produces all types of artwork ranging from traditional decorative art through graphic art to designs for major overseas displays.

There is currently a top level review of all National Government information services which is designed to streamline the whole communications process and make it more effective.

The Policy Secretariat within the Office of Information has been working on proposals for National Government Communications Policy in the broadest possible terms for some time. The combination of the two is expected to resolve many information and communications problems that have been growing in recent years.

General Administrative Services:

Education

The legislative basis for the education system in Papua New Guinea is the Education Act 1970. The Act provides for a National Education System to include Government and church agency schools which meet prescribed conditions in terms of student enrolment and teacher qualifications.

Under the Education Act, the Government financially underwrites all schools within the system by paying teachers' salaries. Schools accept national control over planning and professional staffing matters. Non-government agencies retain supervisory responsibility over their schools and colleges with appropriate staffing safeguards.

Administration and Control

Ultimate authority over all education, including the universities, is exercised by two Ministers: the Minister for Education, Science and Culture and the Minister for Higher Education.

Advising the Minister for Education on policies and plans for the development of the education system is the National Education Board. The board is chaired by the Secretary for Education and comprises representatives from the Government, churches, local government councils, community representatives and teachers. It is responsible for allocating quotas of teachers to provinces and monitoring the operations of the education system.

Administration has been decentralised by the creation of a provincial education board for each province, and a board of management or governing council for each school or institution in the province. Each provincial education board is headed by the Provincial Superintendent and has representatives from various groups in the province.

Administering the conditions of service of teachers is the Teaching Service Commission. The commission is the employing authority for all teaching staff in the National Education System.

In 1976 an amendment was made to the Education Act regarding the power of governing bodies to collect fees from students. The amendment ensured that the National Education Board retained ultimate power over the setting of fees in international schools. Governing bodies are allowed to determine fee levels and collect fees within limits prescribed by the board.

Primary Education

The task of community primary education is to equip the child with basic knowledge, concepts, and skills which will be of use to him in his home community, regardless of whether he proceeds to high school.

In 1978, enrolment in 1 961 community schools was 262 726. In addition a further 5 410 students were enrolled in international primary schools, Total enrolments had increased by about 13 953 over those in 1977.

The long-term objective is universal primary education, and the National Education Plan proposes to make significant moves in this direction by enrolling 82 per cent of the seven-year age group in Grade 1 in 1980 and 92 per cent in 1985. If these targets are realised the imbalance in educational opportunities between provinces and the sexes will be largely removed.

However, with the transfer to the provinces of control over the development of primary education, the achievement of national planning targets, particularly in disadvantaged provinces, will become highly dependent on provincial priorities and resources, supplemented by whatever subsidies the National Government can afford to offer.

The key constraint to major change in primary education is the level of education and training of large numbers of teachers. In 1977 the In-service College again gave priority to upgrading the primary teaching force. About 3 per cent of all primary teachers were able to attend an in-service course.

There were 8 590 primary school teachers in 1978 with a supervisory force of 87 inspectors and 20 curriculum advisors. All community school teachers and their supervisors are Papua New Guineans.

Secondary Education

The aim of secondary education is to

provide adequate preparation for post secondary training courses, direct employment needs and responsible participation in community life. The secondary course is in two stages of two years with 40 per cent of students leaving at the end of Grade 8.

Total enrolment of students in 1978 was 33 015 who were accommodated in 88 high schools, 58 of which were Government operated schools. In the same year 718 students were enrolled in two international high schools.

High school leavers are already exceeding training and employment requirements. An increasing proportion of Grade 8 and Grade 10 leavers will be underemployed and the Education Department shares a responsibility with parents, the community and other agencies to ensure that these school leavers also become useful citizens. Consequently, the stage 1 (Grades 7 and 8) curriculum has been revised to incorporate a substantial proportion of practical skills and agricultural activities in addition to regular academic subjects.

Selection into high school is through a nationwide high school selection examination. Grade 6 community school pupils sit this examination in September of each year. Each community school is allocated a quota of the places available in high schools within its province. All community schools in the same provinces get a proportionate share of high school places.

Modification of curriculum for use in high schools is a continuous process. Development of high schools is now taking them in the direction of a closer relationship with the communities they serve, whether they be urban or rural. Most new high schools have been, and will continue to be, small day high schools constructed with a substantial contribution from local communities. Some boarding schools have become self-sufficient in food supplies and others are encouraged to be self-reliant through agricultural and commercial projects.

National High Schools

The aim of national high schools is to provide an alternative to the preliminary year studies at university and eventually to replace the various preliminary years. National high schools are also of particular value to girls as a preparation for university.

Enrolment for the four national high schools (Sogeri, Keravat, Aiyura and Passam) in 1978 totalled 1 372.

Moves to standardise curricula in national high schools commenced in 1977 and courses of study in Social Science, Maths and English were introduced on a trial basis in 1978.

Although national high schools draw most of their students from adjacent provinces, every province in the country is represented by at least one student in each intake for each school. This policy is consistent with an emphasis on cultural activities, expressive arts and the development of a national pride and identity.

Technical Education

Technical colleges provide training to meet identified manpower needs for semi-skilled and sub-professional technical employment. In 1978 the nine technical colleges, including two secretarial colleges, had a total fulltime enrolment of 2 186 students. These students undertake general secondary courses with some introductory technical studies.

Government policy is to phase general studies out of technical colleges, thus freeing a large number of places for specialist technical training at different levels. This will result in expanded capacities for the present secretarial, trade and technician type courses, many of which are organised on a block release basis.

In addition, the Education Department plans to expand greatly the number of pre-employment technical courses of variable duration, usually 20 or 40 weeks, and catering for Grade 8 and Grade 10 school leavers. PETT students can obtain formal trade qualifications by obtaining employment in an area related to their course and returning to a technical college for prescribed formal extension courses.

The curriculum for all areas of technical studies was recently subjected to a major review in structure and content. This review followed reappraisal of the level of competency of technical college leavers and was undertaken to ensure that the industrial requirements for sub-professional, secretarial and trade employment are maintained.

Courses in technical colleges are developed by trade panels which include industry, commerce representatives and national boards of studies with the assistance of curriculum unit officers.

Manual Arts teacher instructing students at a technical college.

Teacher Education

Of the nine primary teachers colleges in the National Education System seven are conducted by church agencies. In 1978 enrolments in the two-year primary pre-service course totalled 2 046 students.

One teachers college was converted in 1979 to become the sole in-service training institution. The other eight colleges prepare student teachers for a career in community schools. As from 1977 all new entrants to community teachers colleges have a minimum education of Grade 10.

Curriculum revision, through college boards of studies, has focused on the implications of the community school concept as developed in the Education Plan. A principal implication is that teachers will have to be sufficiently adaptive and imaginative to approach their lessons in a different way in different locations, while maintaining standards of attainment in the basic subjects.

Expatriate Education

International schools are available to children whose parents desire overseas-type schooling and are prepared to pay an economic fee. The Government's financial contribution to an international school is about the same level as its operating costs for a Papua New Guinea curriculum school. The difference is made up by parents' contributions.

The Education Department administers preparatory, primary and secondary schools that employ foreign curricula. In 1978 the International Schools Unit administered 34 pre-schools, 36 primary schools, two high schools and two correspondence schools.

Adult and Vocational Education

Various adult education courses have been established to meet community needs. A community secondary education programme has been set up in 33 locations.

Vocational centres provide courses of one or two years duration in basic technical and/or agricultural skills with the object of developing more productive citizens either in the monetary or "informal" sectors of the economy. They are mainly based in rural areas and in 1978, the 89 centres had a total enrolment of 4 176 students.

Various adult education courses have been established to meet community needs. A community secondary education programme has been set up in 33 locations.

Formal correspondence studies in Grades 9 and 10 subjects and the Commerce Certificates are being conducted by the College of External Studies. Plans are underway to include formal correspondence studies in Grades 7 in 1980.

Tertiary Education

The Office of Higher Education advises the Government on post secondary education with a view to meeting the nation's needs for trained manpower and to ensure the balanced development and use of post secondary educational resources. The Office is responsible for advising the University Finance Review Committee on levels of funding to be recommended on behalf of the universities.

There are about 44 institutions at the post secondary level that receive support from the National Budget. Additionally there are approximately 30 other institutions, mainly conducted by various church agencies, actively

The Office of Higher Education recently participated in new course development committees. The main ones were library studies, journalism, magisterial studies and mass communication. The Office was also involved with various committees considering the development of new policy project guidelines in tertiary education for the National Public Expenditure Plan.

Tertiary Scholarships

Scholarships are granted to Grades 10 and 12 leavers for placement in universities and post secondary institutions including the teachers colleges.

Most of the scholarships fall under the National Tertiary Scholarship Scheme administered by the Education Department. The scheme provides students free tuition fees, pocket money, book and equipment allowance, and a return fare home each year where appropriate. The scheme has replaced the wide variety of cadetships, sponsorships, scholarships, traineeships, etc. which has developed over the years.

A number of other scholarships are directed and funded by other government departments, and trust funds for several minor scholarships have been set up by different organisations.

Modern and traditional design blend harmoniously in a building on the University of Technology campus at Lae.

The Major Institutions

The University of Papua New Guinea is one of two main tertiary institutions in the country. The university is being developed on a 405-hectare site near Waigani, 12 kilometres from the centre of Port Moresby and two kilometres from the government administrative centre at Waigani.

The university offers degree courses in agriculture, arts, dentistry, economics, education, law, medicine and surgery, and science. Diploma courses in commerce, journalism, psychology and secondary teaching are also offered. The university has a preliminary year course, intended to bridge the gap between secondary schooling and university study.

The campus comprises lecture rooms, offices, a library, an administrative complex, three lecture theatres, a mess and student union building. Services available to students on campus include counselling, health, chaplaincy, and vacation and graduate job placements.

Total enrolments at the university in 1979 were 1 189 students at the Waigani campus and 541 at the Goroka Secondary Teachers College which became part of the university in 1975.

As well as students from Papua New Guinea, there are students from the Solomon Islands, Nauru, New Hebrides, Kiribati, Indonesia, Tonga, Fiji, Western Samoa, the Philippines, Australia, New Zealand and Britain.

Total staff at the university is 880. The academic staff members are mainly from Africa, Australia, Britain, New Zealand and the United States, while the non-academic staff are predominantly Papua New Guineans.

The second major tertiary institution is the Papua New Guinea University of Technology. It is located on a 200-hectare site, about six kilometres from the city of Lae. The university offers degree courses in engineering, architecture, food technology, accountancy, business studies, forestry, medical technology, computer studies and surveying. Diploma course are offered in cartography, commerce, communications, fisheries technology, survey drafting and surveying.

Major enrolments in 1979 were engineering (293), accounting and business studies (204), telecommunications (121), chemical technology (64) and agriculture (49).

Specialised Institutions

The are a number of specialised training colleges not handled by the Education Department, including the PNG Institute of Administration (formerly Administrative College), Community Teachers Training College, Vudal Agricultural College, Civil Aviation College, Dental College, etc.

These colleges train employees from the public service and private firms, as well as students from other Pacific Islands.

The Institute of Administration is the largest government institution for the job training and further education of its staff of public servants. Located at Waigani near the University of Papua New Guinea, it is attended by staff in training from all government departments and authorities.

Courses offered at the institute cover a very wide range from basic clerical and typing skills and procedures to tertiary level diplomas. Courses include a number of specialist areas such as librarianship, government finance and accounting, local government, statistics and foreign relations. Some courses are short, of a few days length, while others such as the diploma courses run to two yesrs.

Library Service

Library services are administered by the National Library Service whose main function is to maintain the national collection of library material about Papua New Guinea. It is the cataloguing and processing centre for all government libraries, particularly public and school libraries.

In 1978 a new National Library building, an independence gift from Australia, was officially opened at Waigani. Since then collections of books have been presented to the Government of Papua New Guinea by Australia, Britain, the United States, Canada and Japan.

The Film Library, National Archives, School Libraries Office and National Bibliography Unit are all part of the National Library.

A separate postal-lending service supplements the distribution of books throughout the 24 public libraries, eight of which are open fulltime.

A small unit, the PNG Research Collection, collects copies of all works published in or written about Papua New Guinea. This includes books, periodicals, maps, photographs, newspapers, pamphlets, films, posters and particularly government publications.

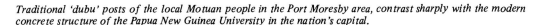

Traditional 'dubu' posts of the local Motuan people in the Port Moresby area, contrast sharply with the modern concrete structure of the Papua New Guinea University in the nation's capital.

Table 1

COMMUNITY SCHOOLS (PAPUA NEW GUINEAN STUDENTS)

	1974	1975	1976	1977	1978
% of 7 year old children in Grade 1	64	68	71	72.7	64
% of 7-12 years olds in all Grades	56	57	58	86.5	56.4
Total enrolment in all Grades	230 445	238 315	255 202	253 608	262 726
Pupil to Teacher rates	31.6	31.4	31.9	30.3	31.3

Table 2

PROVINCIAL HIGH SCHOOL (PAPUA NEW GUINEAN STUDENTS)

	1974	1975	1976	1977	1978
No. of High Schools	73	80	80	82	88
Enrolments	27 220	28 844	30 000	31 426	32 915
Staff	1 160	1 192	1 158	1 185	1 248
Pupil to Teacher rates	23.5	24.2	25.9	26.5	26.4

Table 3

TECHNICAL COLLEGE ENROLMENTS (FULL-TIME PLACES)

	1974	1975	1976	1977	1978
Secondary Students	2 520	2 491	2 100	1 284	429
Trade Courses	329	311	874	847	793
Secretarial	495	555	792	591	622
Art & Craft	40	52	42	4	63
Certificate Courses	172	207	289	205	199
Total Enrolments	3 564	3 616	4 100	2 931	2 106
Staff		263	237	219	202
Pupil to Teacher rates		13.8	17.3	13.4	10.4

Table 4

COMMUNITY TEACHERS' COLLEGES

	1974	1975	1976	1977	1978
Pre-Service Training	1 904	1 990	2 150	1 962	1 802
In-Service	127	145	180	475	154
Total Student Places	2 031	2 135	2 330	2 437	2 046
College Graduates (end of year)	832	857	933	896	912
Staff		166	143	140	127

Table 5

COMMUNITY VOCATIONAL TRAINING CENTRES AND SKULANKAS

	1974	1975	1976	1977	1978
Enrolment, Vocational Centres	4 710	5 000	5 000	4 704	4 176
Enrolment, Skulanka	728	608	500	345	306
Staff, Vocational Centres	246	287	250	248	247
Staff, Skulanka	26	30	15	11	11

SOURCE: DEPARTMENT OF EDUCATION

The modern base hospital at Goroka, Eastern Highlands Province.

Health

Maintenance and improvement of health care services throughout the nation have a major priority in Papua New Guinea. The 1980 National Budget provides K37 million, or 6 per cent of the total budget, for health services. Emphasis has been placed recently on primary health care and increased rural health facilities — more aid posts, more health centres and sub-centres — stressing community health care and self-help.

Hospitals and Health Centres

There are four major hospitals in Papua New Guinea which serve as base hospitals to the four geographic regions — Papua, Highlands, Mainland and New Guinea Islands.

The Port Moresby General Hospital serves the National Capital District and is the referral hospital for the five provinces in the Papuan region — Central, Gulf, Western, Northern and Milne Bay Provinces. The hospital has 632 beds and provides a wide range of specialist services due to its teaching involvement with the Faculty of Medicine of the University of Papua New Guinea. It is equipped with three operating theatres and modern X-ray and pathology facilities. The hospital serves as a training institute for nurses and pathology technicians.

Provincial hospitals are at Kerema, Daru, Popondetta and Alotau, The region has 42 health centres, 61 health sub-centres and 354 aid posts.

The Goroka base hospital, serving provinces in the Highlands region, has 345 beds. It is a modern general hospital with three operating theatres, delivery suites and X-ray and pathology departments.

There are three provincial hospitals — at Mendi, Kundiawa and Mount Hagen. The Highlands region is also served by 39 health centres, 44 health sub-centres and 437 aid posts.

The Angau Memorial Hospital in Lae is the base hospital for the Mainland region. It is a well-equipped hospital with 455 beds, X-ray and laboratory facilities. Attached to the hospital is a modern radiotherapy centre equipped with a Theraton 80 cobalt unit and caesium ward. In this region are three provincial hospitals (Madang, Wewak and Vanimo), one general hospital (Maprik), 54 health centres, 44 health sub-centres and 509 aid posts.

Nonga base hospital serves the town of Rabaul and East New Britain Province. The 400-bed hospital is the referral hospital for West New Britain, New Ireland, Manus and North Solomon Provinces. There are four provincial hospitals — at Kimbe, Kavieng, Lorengau and Arawa — and 31 health centres, 29 health sub-centres and 273 aid posts in the region.

The Mount Hagen hospital in the Western Highlands Province. (Right) an accident victim receives treatment in Port Moresby.

Improvement and Rural Health

The Government is committed to expanding and improving health services to rural areas. Approximately K2.4 million will be allocated among provinces in 1980 for new aid post facilities and staffing. A key element in rural health services is better training for staff, particularly in matters of health education for village communities. Technical assistance will be sought to help prepare a fully integrated programme which extends health services in the most effective way to rural people.

In the next few years a number of major projects as outlined in the 1979-82 National Public Expenditure Plan are expected to be completed. The Mount Hagen Hospital will be upgraded to base hospital standard, and facilities such as a new theatre block, emergency power generator, dental clinic, VD clinic and PABX equipment will be built starting this year.

Major improvements will be made and additional facilities provided at the Port Moresby General Hospital and the Alotau, Popondetta, Angau, Mendi and Vanimo hospitals.

The training programme will get a boost with the construction of an Aid Post Orderlies Training College at Togoba in the Western Highlands Province, the provision of staff and training aids, and the commencement of

Dental services are available from a few private practioners or government operated clinics.

improved training courses in medical technology.

Dental Services

A well equipped dental clinic operates from the grounds of the Port Moresby General Hospital. This provides a school dental service and a general service. The general service is available to all members of the community who are not eligible for registration under the school service or are unable to obtain treatment from private or church practitioners.

Fully equipped dental clinics are located at Alotau, Lae, Madang, Wewak, Goroka, Mount Hagen, Kundiawa, Mendi, Rabaul, Arawa and Buin. School dental clinics, staffed by dental therapists, provide services at the above localities and 33 other centres.

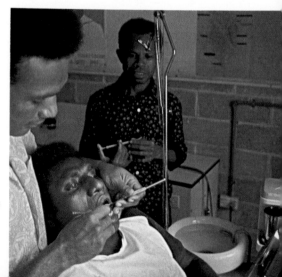

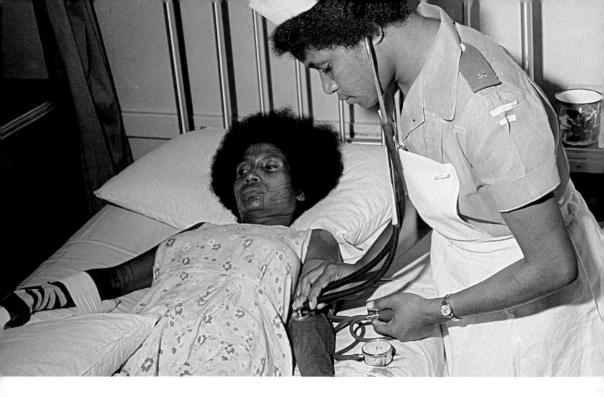

Blood Transfusion Service

This is situated in the grounds of the Port Moresby General Hospital and provides the hospital with blood and blood products, performs tests such as ante-natal checks, and carries out studies on abnormal blood groups, the effects of snake bites, etc. In addition to Port Moresby, blood transfusion services are available at Lae, Madang, Goroka, Rabaul, Wewak, Mount Hagen and Arawa. The service is the responsibility of the Director of the Red Cross Blood Transfusion Service, who is a specialist medical officer.

The Government has allocated funds designed to improve blood transfusion services through the installation of prefabricated cold rooms, the extension of blood transfusion buildings, and purchase of vehicles and equipment for various centres.

Malaria Control

Malaria is an endemic disease in most areas of Papua New Guinea. Twenty years ago, a programme was initiated to control malaria by spraying houses with insecticides, and a considerable degree of success has been achieved in some 13 provinces.

Entomology field teams have been assigned to Vanimo, Kiunga and Daru to study the pattern and prevalence of malaria. Their work will assist greatly in future anti-malarial control measures.

Tuberculosis Control

Tuberculosis is an endemic disease except in the Highlands where, however, its incidence is slowly increasing.

Case finding and vaccination programmes are carried out in all provinces by provincial tuberculosis control officers in health centres and sub-centres. Emphasis is placed on outpatient treatment, as soon as the patient's condition is stabilised, at the nearest aid post or centre.

Leprosy Control

Leprosy is an endemic disease in many parts of the country. Patients receive treatment in wards of general hospital, at outpatients, and from aid posts and health centres. Greater emphasis is now' being placed on domiciliary service and encouraging patients to resume their normal lives since, once treated, they are no longer infectious or a risk to others. Education of staff, patients and the general community is seen as a vital part of the programme.

Two specialist surgeons carry out reconstructive surgery in Papua New Guinea and specialist advice is available from the regional base hospitals.

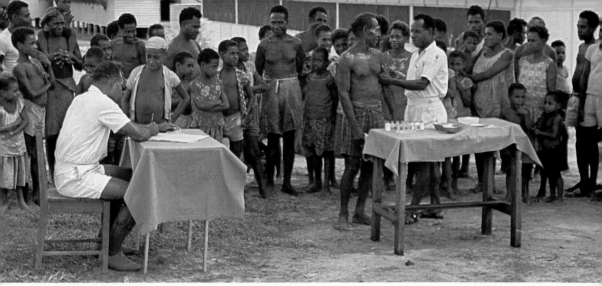

Occasionally mass-vaccination campaigns may have to be mounted and are carried out at regular or special clinics.

Family Health

A comprehensive health service for mothers and children throughout the country is provided. Twenty main centres and 174 rural health centres hold clinics and aid the family planning and nutrition improvement programmes now in operation.

A professional headquarters will be established to oversee the introduction and maintenance of national family planning services. It will also allow the strengthening of family planning inputs into maternal health and child care services as well as health extension programmes at provincial level.

A project design to strengthen the national nutrition programme is also being initiated. New nutrition programmes will be introduced in provinces not yet covered by the programme. In addition, existing services provided by the Health Department will be expanded, improved educational materials will be produced, and support will be provided for existing "Save the Children Fund" personnel in the Highlands region.

Mental Health

Mental health services are designed to provide comprehensive care, treatment, and control of the mentally sick. Such services are provided at the Laloki Psychiatric Centre and Rehabilitation Village Annex in the National Capital District. Mental health services are also available at the Le Hunte Psychiatric Clinic, Port Moresby, and at psychiatric wards of the major general hospitals.

Activities are directed towards supervision of the care and rehabilitation of patients with mental disorders, including treatment of seriously disturbed or criminally insane patients at the Laloki Centre. Also included are out-patient care and supervision at home, counselling families, consultant services and the supervision of patients in general hospitals.

Senior mental health officers maintain contact with other centres through telephone, radio and visits. They are ably assisted by about 30 qualified psychiatric nurses spread throughout the country.

Community psychiatry activities have been an important component of mental health service leading to the reduction of hospitalised patients, many of whom are instead treated at home and on an outpatient basis.

Environmental Health

The environmental health programme is concerned with inspecting and advising on the prevention of pollution, provision of a safe water supply, wholesome food, proper waste disposal facilities, control of disease-bearing insects, etc. The three major health problems in the country (malaria, respiratory diseases and gastro-enteritis) are attributable to an insanitary environment.

Present health programmes are therefore geared to the extension of environmental health facilities particularly to rural areas. Among the more urgent undertakings have been the provision of safe and adequate water and basic sanitation facilities to the villages to prevent the spread of water-borne diseases.

Additional positions of health inspectors

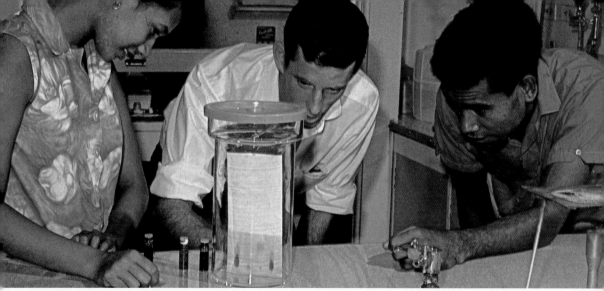

Pathology services are available at the main hospitals and important research has been done especially in conjunction with the blood transfusion service.

have been created to encourage and co-ordinate rural environmental health work. There are now about 90 health inspectors throughout the country, most of whom have been transferred to provincial governments or local government councils.

These include six quarantine officers assigned to carry out full-time inspection work at the six main ports of Port Moresby, Lae, Madang, Rabaul, Vanimo and Kieta.

Some environmental health functions, especially refuse collection and disposal and minor water supply construction have been assumed by local government councils, with health personnel giving advisory and technical assistance.

The construction and maintenance of major environmental health works, like sewerage schemes, waste disposal works and water treatment plants and supply systems for towns are handled by the Department of Works and Supply. Health staff render advisory services on health aspects and implications, as well as standards of treatment.

Considerable assistance is given by the World Health Organisation through the provision of sanitation engineers and consultants who conduct studies, train staff and recommend health guidelines.

Medical Research

The Institure of Medical Research, an independent statutory authority, conducts much of the medical research in Papua New Guinea. The institute receives an annual grant from the Government and can also solicit support from other sources.

Staff of the Faculty of Medicine of the University of Papua New Guinea and the Health Department also engage in medical research and financial support is provided by both bodies. Overseas persons or institutions may conduct medical research projects in the country, but only with the approval of the Minister for Health.

Church Medical Services

Christian missions provide medical and health services through hospitals, health centres, aid posts and field services. The Health Department provides drugs and dressings to approved health establishments as well as financial assistance through transport subsidies, and quarterly grant-in-aid payments based upon the volume of work being carried out by the missions' health establishments.

Pharmaceutical Services

Hospital pharmacies are established at the four base hospitals. In addition, there are pharmacies supervised by supply officers at smaller hospitals in Wewak, Madang and Mount Hagen.

A K290 000 medical store will be constructed over the next two years at Lae to facilitate drug supplies to the Morobe, Madang, Northern, East Sepik and Highlands Provinces.

There are 18 private pharmacies throughout the country. These operate in Port Moresby (seven), Lae (three), Rabaul (two) and one each at Madang, Wewak, Goroka, Mount Hagen, Kavieng and Kieta.

Welfare and Recreation

Responsibility for implementing government policies on social welfare rests with the Office of Home Affairs.

The Government's key areas of interests have been child welfare, rehabilitation of young offenders, increased facilities for the disabled, and repatriation and grants to needy families.

Child Welfare

Child welfare services are concerned with administering and rehabilitating wards sentenced to juvenile institutions, the care and placement of adopted or neglected children, and supervision of operations of child-minding centres.

Young people who are either first offenders or have been involved in minor offences are usually placed on probation under the guidance of welfare officers. These youth stay in their own communities with their parents or guardians but are required to report to social workers regularly for a period ranging from two to six months or more.

Wards are young people under 16 who are regularly in conflict with the law or have committed serious offences. Once a child is declared a ward, he or she is sent to juvenile institution with the aim of rehabilitation.

There are four main juvenile institutions in the country: Boys Town in Wewak, Togatia House near Goroka, and Veimauri Children's Village and Red Shield Training Centre both in the Central Province. All four institutions are owned and run by non-government organisations, in particular the Catholic Church and the Red Cross. The Government contributes in terms of grants-in-aid made through the Office of Home Affairs.

There are 48 child-minding centres throughout the country, and welfare officers carry out follow up visits and inspections of these centres every three months to ensure that children receive a satisfactory standard of care.

Social Services

The social services provided are child allowances, ex-gratia allowances, grants-in-aid and repatriation.

Child allowances are issued to destitutes or children with no sufficient means of support due to either the parents being deceased, in prison or wife being deserted.

Ex-gratia allowances are granted to deprived families on the grounds of genuine hardships especially where there are no means of support in the community due to a breakdown in the family or clan structure.

There are two kinds of grants-in-aid. One is paid to social workers at approved child welfare institutions, including the Cheshire Homes Family Services. The other is paid to voluntary organisations which apply for such grants. A total amount of K145 000 was paid out as grants to 22 organisations last year, and this amount is being increased.

The social welfare repatriation programme involves assisting destitutes who cannot afford to travel back to their home provinces. Assistance in this matter is granted only as a last resort, that is, after attempts have been made in getting clan and family members to assist in meeting the expenses.

A National Board for the Disabled has been established as a result of a study and recommendations made by a United Nations Development Programme advisor. The board is responsible for liaising and co-ordinating between the agencies currently caring and providing services for the disabled and the Government. The board comprises welfare, education, health and labour officers as well as representatives from disabled bodies.

Problems associated with alcoholism and causes and effects of prostitution also come under the concern of the Office of Home Affairs. While the gravity of the problem in both areas has been recognised, no studies or policy proposals have been made due to lack of staff and funds.

Recreation and Sports

Sport in Papua New Guinea has grown in the number of clubs and associations actively engaged in town competitions and in the number of people in rural areas taking part in organised games. The most popular sports are rugby league, soccer, Aussie Rules, basketball and volleyball.

Facilities are gradually improving although not yet adequate to meet the ever-increasing demand from the public for sports and recreational activities.

The government agency responsible for

Two of Papua New Guinea's international class boxing champions. John Aba (right) with Martin Beni and his Commonwealth championship belt.

promoting the development of sports in Papua New Guinea is the Division of Sports and Recreation of the Office of Home Affairs. One of the division's main concerns at present is the provision of guidance and advice in areas of administration and self-help fund-raising.

Significant activities and achievements in 1978 included the creation of the National Sports Training Institute Board of Trustees, the appointment of the Third National Sports Council, the inauguration of the PNG Sports Aid Federation and the visit of a UNESCO consultant on physical education and sport.

The National Sports Council, the advisor and

policy maker on sports and recreation, has issued a set of guidelines aimed at bringing about improved organisation and discipline in all sporting bodies. Under the guidelines, the country's different sports governing bodies will accept responsibility for the operations of their member associations and clubs so that sports in the country will develop free of unsportsmanlike practices and behaviour.

The National Sports Training Institute assists sporting bodies with their administrative, coaching, refereeing and sports medicine. The Sports Aid Foundation, on the other hand, supports the fund-raising activities of sporting

Whether competing in international events . . .

. . . or in a domestic match, Papua New Guineans give sport an important place in their daily life.

organisations with subsidies to foster the growth and improvement of top level sport. Thus, while the Recreation Division concentrates on the establishment of a broad village and community sports' base, the foundation supports athletes in high performance levels.

Sporting bodies in Papua New Guinea have been striving to reach higher standards in particular sports, and last year took part in a number of overseas sporting events. The most notable participation was at the Commonwealth Games in Edmonton, Canada where boxer Tumat Sogolik became the first ever Papua New Guinean to win a Games medal.

The national junior soccer team took part for the first time in the World Junior Football Tournament and performed with credit displaying much potential for future development. The women's table tennis team placed third in the Oceania Championships, and the Goroka netball association did well in sports competitions during the Solomon Islands independence celebrations.

There are no plans to give priority consideration in resource allocation to various sports which do not attract large gate takings or do not have access to overseas expertise. This is designed to bring all sports up to a balanced development level.

Housing and
Urban Development

Much of the residential housing construction in the urban areas of Papua New Guinea is the responsibility of the National Housing Commission, a statutory body of the Government. Apart from the commission, there are a number of private developers who construct, sell and let or lease out flats, detached and town houses.

In the rural areas villagers construct their own houses largely using traditional building materials, designs and techniques. Much of village housing construction is carried out individually or by village groups. There has been little attempt to organise large-scale construction at the village level.

The Department of Works and Supply is another government construction agency which has been building houses for public servants. Houses, flats, SOQs and hostels built by the department are managed and maintained by another government body, the Department of Urban Development. Houses for public servants are let out at highly subsidised rates, unlike charges levied by the National Housing Commission which are intended to recoup all costs put into land development and housing construction.

Housing rates range from K4 a week for single bedroom accommodation to K200 for an executive multi-bedroom house. Sale prices for houses and flats vary from location to location. Prospective buyers may expect to pay a minimum of K5 000 for a fully serviced but unfurnished accommodation.

At present there is no government control on rents or sale prices of houses and flats. Prevailing prices are therefore determined by the interaction of supply and demand. There are now more than 5 000 registered applicants for accommodation throughout the country. The Government is examing all possible ways to reduce this demand.

National Housing Commission

The Government's urban housing programme dates back to 1968 when the National Housing Commission was set up by virtue of the Housing Commission Act 1967. The commission was created to provice public housing programmes, promote self-help housing and encourage home ownership.

Since its inception the commission has acquired land, developed it and built houses and flats for more than 7 000 families. In addition, it has been involved in developing recreational facilities, shops, schools and other community services.

The commission had the initial task of building and renting for low income earners, particularly public servants. Later on, tenants had the option of buying their houses from the commission after two years of tenancy.

In 1973 the commission started running self-help building schemes for urban settlers. The schemes were designed to help rural migrants adapt to city living. The commission subdivided land into allotment blocks and provided settlers with cash grants, loans and advice to build their own houses. It also built stores and community centres in the settlement areas.

Community-based housing construction programmes are continuing but over the past five years have been hampered by financial limitations and land unavailability. In the 18 months from June 1977 to December 1978, the commission built a total of 1 079 houses of which about two-thirds were rental housing, indicating the increasingly high demand for rental housing.

Urban Development

The Department of Urban Development was set up in 1978 to take overall responsibility for the Government's urban development policies. The department was given responsibility for all non-commercial aspects of government housing as well as town planning, self-help housing and overall urban development policy. With the creation of the department, the National Housing Commission became a fully commercial housing authority.

Present government policy is to encourage home ownership by selling its own stock of houses to current tenants. Over the next five years, it will rationalise rents across the country, making it relatively more expensive to rent compared with buying a house.

In selling government pool houses first priority is given to the present legal tenants, and other public servants come next. To purchase a government house, one can make an outright purchase or pay fortnightly instalments of K46 for a period of 10 years, two months.

The Government recently approved loan guarantee schemes for housing concurrently with sales of pool housing. The loan guarantee scheme aims to assist citizens, particularly in rural areas, to obtain credit for building or purchasing their own houses. Loan guarantees are provided to a maximum loan of K10 000 with provision for 15 per cent cost over-run giving a maximum of K11 500 in total. The maximum period of loan for which the Government will provide a guarantee will generally be 15 years, and interest rate will be the bank's normal rate.

The Government has now adopted the principle that public subsidies for formal housing and government responsibility for housing its employees should be phased out. Another government target is to make available adequate supply of land for housing development, based on fair and equitable agreements between owners and potential users of land.

Emphasis in the office accommodation programme will be to locate government departments centrally at the Waigani City Centre and closely as possible to related functions. New office buildings will be limited to three floors walk-up with sub-basement car parking.

The Department of Urban Development will continue carrying out minor studies and revisions to develop realistic development programmes for urban areas. Studies will include land development needs in all urban centres for residential, industrial and commercial activities, housing needs, urban household surveys, urban traffic surveys, etc.

Electricity

Electricity in Papua New Guinea is supplied by the Papua New Guinea Electricity Commission, a statutory body established in 1963.

The commission took over the generation and distribution of electricity in the country from the Australian Administration, which had been administering electricity supply in Papua New Guinea since World War II.

The commission operates under the Ministry of Public Utilities but is autonomous and functions as a commercial and service organisation. Its overall operation involves investiga-

tions, generation, transmission and distribution of electricity.

Organisation

The commission at present owns and operates power stations in 25 urban areas of the country. There are four major hydro-electric stations of which the newest is the Ramy hydro-plant near Kainantu, Eastern Highlands. The installed capacity of Ramu is 45 MW, which supplements the Highlands towns and the two coastal townships of Madang and Lae.

The National Capital District is serviced by the Rouna 1, 2 and 3 hydro-plant complex which has an installed capacity of 49 MW.

Two major hydro-schemes are currently under development. They are Rouna 4 along the Laloki River, which will cater Port Moresby's increasing electricity demand, and Warangoi, East New Britain, to supply Rabaul.

Other centres are supplied by diesel power stations with an installed capacity of 42.02 MW. In addition, the commission maintains on behalf of the Government 140 minor diesel stations on a non-profit basis. These stations are usually small government centres where power is supplied mainly as an inducement for officers to work in these areas.

The Rouna Falls on the Laloki River thunders down from the Sogeri Plateau to the coastal plain near Port Moresby when its waters are not generating power for the nation's capital.

The holding weir at Rouna No. 2 on the Laloki river diverts water to an underground power station 150 metres below the surface.

Rural Electrification

The Government has adopted a rural electrification policy designed at extending electric power to most rural areas based on supply from small hydro sets. The main thrust of the rural electrification programme is the construction of large numbers of small hydro schemes — most of them without dams and based on "run-of-the-river" flows only — close to appropriate load centres throughout the country.

The first steps towards rural electrification were taken in 1975 with the formation of a Provincial Electrification Division within the Electricity Commission and the sending of commission officers overseas to study the subject. At the same time, experts on rural electrification from the United States were invited to survey various areas of Papua New Guinea and to recommend a suitable electrification programme for the country.

The electrification programme received a big boost in 1977 when the Asian Development Bank approved a loan for the establishment of four small hydro schemes (Kimbe, Namatanai, Bialla and Tinputz) at a total cost of K3.3 million. These schemes are expected to be followed by other projects, particularly in Wabag, Popondetta and Manus.

National Policy

The Government has now adopted a policy on the development and expansion of electricity supply throughout Papua New Guinea. Under this policy, the Electricity Commission is directed to achieve rural electrification and extend supply of electricity by construction of provincial hydro schemes and large hydro schemes where feasible. It is also directed to utilise other forms of energy where appropriate in association with the energy policy for Papua New Guinea.

In January 1979 the Government authorised the commission to take over complete responsibility for national electrification. Six months later, it gave the commission approval to construct major and provincial hydro-electricity schemes to allow extension of supply to rural areas. The cost of the hydro schemes in the National Public Expenditure Plan is more than K100 million.

The major hydro schemes included in the NPEP programme are Rouna 4, Upper Warangoi, Kaugel in the Southern Highlands and Luwini in Oro Province.

Transmission and Supply

The transmission system in Papua New Guinea generally consists of single circuit 66 kV transmission lines with major zone sub-stations to service larger towns and nearby areas. Distribution voltages are mainly 11 kV and 22 kV; 33 kV is also used. The 22 kV level is used predominantly in rural areas, with single-phase and S.W.E.R. extensions to small consumers.

The supply is 50 hertz alternating current, normally at 220/240 volts single phase, or 415/440 volts three-phase.

The commission is using the Standard Association of Australia Wiring Rules as a guide for the standard of Papua New Guinea. The country is standardised on a 415/240V Multiple-Earthed-Neutral system, with an earth wire run to all metal encased appliances.

Training

Education and training of young Papua New Guineans is of major importance in the commission's plans for advancement of national officers.

With the establishment of a training complex in Port Moresby, the commission has a supply of young men in training to occupy positions as clerks, draftsmen, welders, linesmen, power station operators, diesel mechanics, etc. Selected trainees are given cadetship to attend the University of Papua New Guinea, the PNG University of Technology or institutions in Australia for degree or diploma couses in engineering and surveying.

The intensive training programme has given nationals an opportunity to fill senior positions and progressively take over technical fields within the commission.

A mass of coloured cables is fed into a wiring duct during the construction of a power project.

The scene at the official opening of the first stage of the Ramu River Power Project in the Eastern Highlands Province. This power project supplies electricity to highlands towns and the two coastal centres of Lae and Madang.

ELECTRICITY STATISTICS

	1973	1974	1975	1976	1977	1978
Generating Plant Installed (Kilowatts)	74 700	85 440	83 946	126 482	127 712	127 903
Kilowatt-hours Generated (Millions)	243.546	259.893	289.257	314.952	334.055	413.771
Number of Ultimate Consumers	23 674	24 763	26 675	28 410	30 090	33 031
Ultimate Consumption (kwh millions)	213.07	231.57	289.26	273.99	302.94	305.24
Revenue from Sales of Electricity (Millions)	8.397	9.049	11.254	15.087	18.839	17.085
Expenditure (Millions)	6.952	8.952	10.775	12.447	14.034	28.981

SOURCE; ELECTRICITY COMMISSION

Water Supply and Sewerage

The water resources of Papua New Guinea represent one of the country's major assets. It has been estimated that it shares with Nepal the position of having the only potentially exportable hydro-electric power capacity in the world. This position is brought about by three closely interrelated factors: very high rainfall, high runoff and steep mountains.

While the country has vast scope for the development of hydro power, the principal limitation lies in the availability of markets. The country's identified hydro power potential is currently estimated at between 20 000 and 25 000 MW.

There are numerous large rivers and many more smaller streams, many large enough to provide water supplies to towns without impounded storage. Many streams however carry a high sediment load as a result of natural erosion of the young topography.

The quality of water is generally good except for the silt problem already mentioned. The population is scattered and pollution is generally slight except in the more closely settled areas of the Highlands.

Groundwater is frequently found and springs occur. Some urban areas like Port Moresby, Lae, Madang, Rabaul, Kimbe have developed groundwater to a small degree. Lae, the biggest user, is supplied with about 3 520 cubic metres per day from ground water reservoirs. Due to the abundance of surface water over most of the country groundwater resources have been explored and developed only to a very limited extend.

Urban Water Supply

The Government recognises the importance of adequate potable water supplies and safe hygienic disposal of sewage to the health of its people and as a prerequisite to industrial and commercial development.

Fully reticulated water supplies are provided

Water spilling over the Sirinumu dam on the Laloki river regulates supply to the Rouna complex of power stations downstream as well as the city water reticulation system of Port Moresby.

in Port Moresby, Goroka, Popondetta, Arawa and Alotau. In addition, water supply systems are partially existing or under construction in Kavieng, Daru, Lae, Rabaul, Namatanai, Vanimo, Kupiano, Wewak, Madang, Mount Hagen, Bulolo, Wabag, Kwikila and Kainantu. Supplies in these towns are expected to be fully operational by 1981.

Port Moresby has a comprehensive reticulated water system. The water supply is taken from the Laloki River, which is regulated by the Sirinumu Dam for the generation of power at a chain of generating stations.

Four major water supply projects — at Lae, Wewak, Mount Hagen and Madang — are being financed with the assistance of the Asian Development Bank. Total expenditure · on water supply for these towns is estimated to total K22 million over the next four years. Water supply at Wabag is being financed by a loan from the Japanese Overseas Economic Cooperation Board. A team of experts from the World Bank and the World Health Organisation recently appraised water supply systems and sanitation in Papua New Guinea, and both organisations have indicated interest in assisting future projects, particularly in smaller urban settlements and rural areas.

To ensure efficient and reliable supply of potable water the Government is liaising with consultants from the Asian Development Bank in working out financial and management policies for water supplies. The study, which also includes sewage and sanitation, will be completed in 1979.

The present administration of water supplies is shared by the National, Provincial and Local Governments. As a result charges vary throughout the country but are generally within the range of 10 to 15 toea per thousand litres. The present review being undertaken is likely to result in a uniform economic charge of 30 to 40 toea per thousand litres.

Rural Supplies

There is an ongoing project in four Highlands provinces for the construction of simple water supply systems and pit latrines in 144 villages. A significant aspect of the project is to encourage villagers to accept responsibility for and understand maintenance requirements of simple water supply systems. It is anticipated that the project will have an important demonstration effect and will result in villagers becoming increasingly aware of the benefits of having safe and convenient water supplies and waste disposal facilities.

A similar project to survey water supplies and the use of existing facilities will start this year in Morobe and Central Provinces. The project aims to examine villagers' attitudes to and understanding of water supply problems and to reduce wastage in the provision of water supplies.

Fire Services

The administration of fire services is carried out by the Fire Services Branch of the Department of Public Utilities. The branch is headed by the Chief Fire Officer who is directly responsible to the Secretary for Public Utilities.

There are 12 fire stations throughout Papua New Guinea — three in the National Capital District, and one each at Lae, Popondetta, Mount Hagen, Goroka, Wewak, Madang, Rabaul, Kavieng and Arawa. The Fire Services Branch has a staff of 170 men manning these stations.

The vehicle fleet comprises 21 fire tenders, including two newly-acquired fire trucks. The new appliances are water carriers of 800 gallon capacity, fitted with pumps capable of delivering between 500-700 gallons per minute at pressures of at least 150 pounds per square inch. They are expected to be the first in a continuing programme of replacing old machines in use.

As well as fire-fighting, the Fire Services Branch spends time in preventive work, educating people about fire risks and basic fire prevention techniques. Fire officers conduct regular lectures/demonstrations in hospitals, schools and other establishments on fire safety and basic functions of fire-fighting. The branch also investigates possible fire hazards and recommends safety measures at the request of house or building owners.

Improving the Service

Various programmes and projects are currently being implemented to increase the efficiency of the national fire service.

A training programme consisting of courses in basic firemanship as well as officer training has been initiated. Nine courses will be held in

Though no major aircraft fire has had to be attended to date, airport firefighters at Port Moresby have regular 'dry runs' on a simulated aircraft fire near the airport.

1979 to train present staff as well as new recruits. Ninety recruits were admitted this year, some of whom have completed training and have been posted to different centres.

The increase in the number of high-rise buildings in Port Moresby has necessitated the training of firemen in fire-fighting techniques in large and multi-storey buildings. Firemen are now learning about fixed protection systems in buildings and how they could be used in conjunction with an appliance like the snorkel.

The snorkel is a truck with a two-elbowed arm which has a working height of up to 96 feet. It has been recommended for use in Port Moresby because it is suitable for fire-fighting and rescue work in large factories, supermarket stores or buildings up to eight storeys high.

With the assistance of an expert from Australia, an intensive study of all aspects of fire-fighting services in Papua New Guinea was completed recently and recommendations to upgrade the services were put on paper.

Police

The Royal Papua New Guinea Constabulary is responsible for the preservation of peace and order and the enforcement of the law in Papua New Guinea.

The Constabulary has a long proud history, dating back to the year 1888 when the first police force was formed by the old German administration in Rabaul. Two years later the British New Guinea Armed Constabulary was established in Port Moresby. Later these two forces became the New Guinea Police Force and the Royal Papuan Constabulary respectively.

During World War II the two forces were joined and many policemen fought on the side of the Allies. In 1952 the joint force was named the Royal Papua and New Guinea Constabulary, a title that was not changed until 1972, when the "and" was dropped. The Constabulary is now one of the few police forces in the world allowed to use the word "Royal" in its official title.

Organisation

The Police Force is headed by the Commissioner of Police who is responsible for the superintendence, efficient organisation and control of the Force. Directly under the Commissioner is the Deputy Commissioner and below them are five Assistant Commissioners (Personnel, Logistics, Operations, Criminal Investigation, and Research and Development).

In 1978 the Constabulary was reorganised into four regional commands to give more effective support to provincial forces through decentralisation of authority to the regions. Each regional division is under the command of a divisional superintendent; the provinces comprising each region are in turn headed by provincial police commanders.

'A' Division is the Papua Region with head-quarters at Port Moresby. This division includes Central, Gulf, Western, Northern and Milne Bay Provinces.

'B' Division is the Highlands Region with headquarters at Mount Hagen. It covers Western Highlands, Southern Highlands, Enga, Chimbu and Eastern Highlands Provinces.

'C' Division is the New Guinea Coastal Region comprising Morobe, Madang, East Sepik and West Sepik Provinces. Division headquarters at Lae.

'D' Division is the New Guinea Islands Region, with headquarters at Rabaul, and covering East New Britain, West New Britain, New Ireland, Manus and North Solomons Provinces.

Crime

During the past year 59 335 crimes were reported to the police. Most of the crimes reported were offences against property and good order (break and enter, stealing, unlawful use of vehicles, riotous behaviour). Another major group reported was offences against the person, which include assault, use of violence, murder, etc. A total of 49 798 arrests were made by the police during the same period.

Excessive consumption of alcohol has played a major role in many cases of violent crimes, as has the following of traditional values in exacting compensation.

Policemen may serve under widely varying conditions, from a remote rural patrol post (above) to the front seat of a traffic control vehicle in the nation's capital, Port Moresby.

Traffic

Economic progress has in recent years resulted in a significant increase in the number of vehicles and of drivers throughout Papua New Guinea. Unfortunately there has been a corresponding, if not bigger, increase in the number of traffic accidents.

A total of 6 220 accidents were reported last year, resulting in 224 people being killed and 1 757 being injured. In many accidents, liquor was a contributing factor. Another major factor was the use of defective motor vehicles.

Road safety activities of the Police Force concentrate on a series of education campaigns in schools and other institutions. School lectures are conducted regularly to give children a good knowledge of pedestrian safety leading to an awareness of the need for road safety and good driving techniques in later life. In addition, training of traffic policemen continues with courses at Bomana Police College and on-the-job experience.

The Central Traffic Registry has come under the control of the Department of Transport and Civil Aviation which is now responsible for the control of driver licensing, registration of vehicles, and the roadworthiness inspection system. The Police Force plays an important role in upholding the law covering these three areas.

Mobile Force

The Police Mobile Force consists of specially-trained and equipped mobile squads which deal with serious disturbances, operate against rioters, and carry out protective and control operations.

The primary role of the Mobile Force involves tasks associated with civil unrest and internal security. Secondary role duties include crowd control, support for police station personnel, anti-vagrancy operations, search and rescue, etc.

Mobile squads of a type were first introduced into the Constabulary in 1962 as a result of the Buka riots in Bougainville. In 1966 the first full time mobile squad was formed at the Police College, Bomana. Initial training of the mobile squads were based on the operation of similar units in the Fiji Police Force. This training has been updated to relate to conditions and experiences in various places within Papua New Guinea.

Police dogs are used in the apprehension of criminals on urban patrols.

The Mobile Force has assumed an increasingly active role in recent years, particularly in incidents involving tribal fighting. It has also been actively deployed in connection with large scale brawls, support to small police patrols under attack, demonstration and protest marches, and inter-group disputes.

Field uniforms and poly-carbonate riot shields are an integral part of the gear for members of the Mobile Force. Trials and surveys are presently being carried out on rubber bullets, tear gas equipment and the latest anti-riot and non-lethal weapons.

Sector Patrol

The Sector Patrol system was introduced in the National Capital District in 1976 to provide continuous mobile patrolling throughout the various sectors of the city. The patrol comprises 214 policemen and 26 specially-designed vehicles.

The sector patrol has helped reduce urban crime, particularly breaking and entering, and has resulted in an increase in arrests for a variety of offences. In recent months, however, it has encountered problems caused by rapid turnover of patrol officers and the fast growth of the city in relation to patrol work loads.

A review of the sector patrol system is currently being held, with assistance from the South Australian Police Force. The review will analyze sector work loads and the functions of the operations room at Central Police Station. Four national officers will be trained to act as permanent staff for the operations room.

Logistics

The Logistics Branch is responsible for the administration of the police works programme and accommodation, and the acquisition and control of stores, equipment, vehicles and radio communications.

In recent years progress has been made in providing the Constabulary with new equipment.

Steps are being taken to raise the standard of police housing. Major housing projects costing almost K1 million have been built at Kila Barracks, Kerowagi Mobile Squad Depot and Wewak Barracks.

A number of police stations have been opened or are under construction at Kwikila, Bulolo, Walium, Popondetta, Mendi, Aitape, Kimbe, Buin and Panguna.

Manning

The Constabulary has an actual strength of 342 officers and 4 395 constables, below combined authorised establishment strength of 5 887.

The Police Force experiences a high rate of wastage or loss of personnel and recruitment has not been sufficiently high enough to increase the police strength.

Continuing efforts are being made to attract suitable recruits and new and better recruiting methods are being employed. These and improved education facilities at the Police

Participation in daily flag raising and lowering ceremonies on rural patrol posts is a familiar sight. Villagers generally stop by to watch and the smart parade movements of the policemen, emphasising their discipline and efficiency, never fails to impress the onlookers.

College are expected to produce a good class of recruits and make up for the wastage of previous years.

An innovation in the Force was the recruitment of the first policewomen in mid 1977. Woman constables undergo six months training after which they assume duties as communications operators or criminal investigators in addition to their work with the female and juvenile sections.

Training

The main training establishments are the Police College at Bomana, the Joint Services College at Lae, and the Mobile Force Training Depot at Tomaringa in East New Britain.

Training receives high priority in the Constabulary and considerable use has been made of other training institutions within Papua New Guinea and overseas.

A comprehensive training programme known as Phase Development Plans has been drawn up to increase police incentive and morale and thereby promote efficiency within the Force.

The plan lays out in phases the career prospects of both officers and constables. Each phase is divided into three parts — training period, work experience, then review and assessment. At the completion of all phases, officers will have served a total of 32 years and constables a total of 28 years.

The first part of the plan has been completed and initial results are now being assessed.

Applicants to the Force undergo tight screening and have to pass a series of tests. Successful ones go through four months' basic training at Bomana after which they are posted to a police station as probationary constables for one year's practical training.

Training for recruits at the Police College consists of courses in police law, police practice, social science and psychology, physical education, self-defence, basic arms drill and first aid.

In addition to basic training, the College provides special training for officers of all ranks. This includes courses related to detective training, prosecution, basic investigation and driving.

Combined performances of the Police, Corrective Services and Defence Force bands are a feature on many official functions.

Public Relations

An active campaign is maintained to keep both the public and members of the Constabulary aware of developments in areas of police involvement. The public relations exercise concentrates on gaining public co-operation to combat lawlessness.

Lectures and film screenings are conducted regularly by the public relations office with the co-operation of police commanders in various areas. Lectures stress the need for public co-operation in crimefighting and the necessity for children to be given a sound knowledge of and respect for the laws of the land.

A good relationship has been established with both the local and overseas media through daily press briefings and regular press conference with senior police officers.

Other public relations activities consist of assistance given to recruitment through displays and materials for careers weeks, shows, etc., and photographic coverage for important ceremonies, parades and presentations.

Police Band

The main functions of the Police Band are to entertain the people of Papua New Guinea and to provide musical accompaniment for parades and other police ceremonies.

The Band has featured prominently in past Independence celebrations and visits of various foreign dignitaries. It conducts regular performances in schools and other institutions and performs radio broadcasts in order to foster good relations between the public and the Police Force.

Training for Band members is continuous and includes instrumental techniques, elementary harmony, marching routine and melodic dictation. Achievements in recent years include hundreds of public and school concerts, numerous recordings for the NBC, concerts for tourist ships, guards of honours, tours by sea, and performances overseas such as at the Tasmania Military Tatoo.

Task Force Review

A Police Task Force was formed in 1976 to carry out a thorough and wide ranging study of all aspects of the work of the Constabulary and to report on the requirements needed by the Police Force to carry out its duties.

The report of the Task Force was completed recently and recommended the development of a much more sophisticated and skilled Police Force in Papua New Guinea.

The report pointed out that the Constabulary had expanded mainly in town areas but had not developed throughout the nation as a whole. The Constabulary was quite unable to provide more than the minimum standard of service because the increase in population was outstripping the capabilities of the Police Force.

Through Government support, a plan would be developed to bring the Force up to an unacceptable level as soon as finance and manpower were available.

Corrective Institutions

Corrective institutions have been operating in Papua New Guinea as part of the police forces since the early 20th century.

However, it was only in 1957 that the first Commissioner for Corrective Institutions was named. He had responsibility for Bomana, the only corrective institution then existing in the country.

Today the Commissioner is responsible for 23 institutions and an establishment of 1 500 warders (Assistant Correctional Officers) and 100 Correctional Officers.

History

The Corrective Institutions Branch came into existence in 1957 when the Corrective Institutions Ordinance came into effect. While Bomana was the only institution administered by the branch at that time, there were more than 150 other "institutions" around the country staffed and run by the Police and the Department of Native Affairs.

In 1959 a development programme was started, and some police officers and constables were transferred to the branch, along with a few others who were recruited. By 1969, 14 institutions were being fully administered by the branch.

The branch was recognised in 1971 and its name changed to Corrective Institutions Service. Its stated functions were the safe custody and detention of prisoners sentenced by the Courts, and the correction and rehabilitation of detainees.

Establishment

Of 23 corrective institutions in Papua New Guinea, two are classified as major central institutions. These are Bomana, Port Moresby, and Baisu, near Mount Hagen, the major prison for the Highlands region.

There are 10 central, eight major area and three minor area institutions. Although there has been considerable reduction in the number of institutions from a high 150 in the late 1950s, there are plans to close further smaller institutions. The move is aimed at improving prison security and uplifting conditions of prisoners.

Responsibility for the administration and development of corrective institutions rests with the Corrective Institutions Service. The Service is headed by a Commissioner who is directly responsible to the Secretary for Justice and the Minister for Corrective Institutions.

Rehabilitation and Training

The Corrective Institutions Service gives considerable emphasis on training prisoners in productive skills so that they may become useful citizens when they return to their communities.

Training in specialised trades is provided at seven central institutions. Detainees in smaller institutions are employed in vegetable gardens and in maintenance of work within the institution.

Various fields of training are available to all detainees with the type of training dependent upon terms of sentence.

Every year, around 16 000 people in Papua New Guinea are imprisoned for terms ranging from several days to life. At any one time however, there are only about 4 500 detainees in prison, most of whom are serving short sentences (less than six months) and therefore cannot be trained properly. Thus, only about 400 long-term detainees throughout the country receive some form of training in prisons.

The Bomana Corrective Institution provides training in industrial and agricultural fields. Industrial training is divided into electrical, mechanical, brickmaking, carpentry, joinery, welding, plumbing, signwriting, woodcraft and small industries sections. Agricultural training includes cattle, piggery, poultry, gardening and plantation farming projects.

The biggest training section is in education joinery which turns out desks, stools and other furniture for schools. Equally productive are the agricultural sections which provide a major part of the food needs of institutions.

The Service at present does not maintain a follow up programme on former prisoners so it is not known exactly how many prisoners find employment utilising skills acquired in prison. But a number of ex-prisoners are known to have found jobs as carpenters, joiners, plaster-makers, mechanics and electricians. Other prisoners, particularly those in the highlands, make good use of agricultural methods learned and have set up their own farm projects.

Youth and Female Offenders

Of the 16 000 people jailed in Papua New Guinea every year, about eight per cent or 1 200 are young offenders (under 18 years). The Government recognises the importance of youth rehabilitation centres as a means of separating juveniles from older criminals and has given more support for rehabilitative rather than retributive treatment to young offenders.

In 1979 grants of K10 000 each were given for the improvement of youth rehabilitation centres in Wewak, Goroka, Sogeri and Bereina. Approval has also been given for the establishment of a K79 000 youth detainee centre at Lae.

Corrective institutions accommodate about 300 female prisoners of which about 100 are long-term. Many of the long-term prisoners are detained at the Bomana Female Section where they receive training in different activities such as sewing, handcraft and gardening.

Rights and Benefits

Detainees receive benefits like religious guidance, recreational activities, regular health check up, and family visit privileges while in prison.

Every prisoner undergoes a complete medical check up before imprisonment and upon release. In between, he gets regular X-ray and dental check ups. Serious physical or mental cases are brought to hospitals.

Religious services are conducted regularly in the institutions and chaplains are available on call. Prisoners also get the chance to participate in sports and see movies. They are entitled to visits from immediate members of their family twice a month. Occasionally, welfare officers visit detainees to determine their needs and problems and to offer counselling advice.

Prisoners enjoy other rights under the Standard Minimum Rules for the Treatment of Detainees and the International Covenants of Human Rights. Thus, they are not employed on projects outside prisons whereby they come into contact with the public and are subjected to shame or embarrassment.

Review of Institutions

In August 1978, the Minister for Corrective Institutions set up an Interdepartmental Advisory Committee to review the work of the Corrective Institutions Service. The committee visited major institutions and observed working conditions and training of staff, food supply and living conditions of prisoners, rehabilitation programmes, and relationship between detainees and staff. They gathered views of correctional officers, interested persons and bodies, and to a lesser extent, detainees.

The committee completed its report recently and made a number of recommendations.

The main thrust of the report is toward self-reliance, rehabilitation and proper staff conditions. It recommends prisoners be made to do more productive work so they would become less of a drain on the national economy. It also calls for regionalisation of many functions to get stores and supplies more quickly to institutions. Prison staff should be given more training and provided with better working and housing conditions, the report added.

Defence

The Papua New Guinea Defence Force is unified and does not consist of separate Army, Navy or Air Force components. However, identifiable within the Defence Force are three operational elements — land, maritime and air — which in turn are supported by supply, transport, maintenance and training elements.

The Defence Force evolved from the former Australian Services — navy, army and air force — which had previously operated independently in Papua New Guinea.

On 26 January 1973 the Papua New Guinea Defence Force was established with headquarters at Murray Barracks in Port Moresby. The Force was manned by 3 500 uniformed personnel, both Australian and Papua New Guinean of the three Australian Services. By Independence in 1975, the present Commander, Brigadier General E.R. Diro had become the first Papua New Guinean to command the Force. At the same time, the three services merged into a single Defence Force.

Policies and Functions

Papua New Guinea is located in an archipelagic chain at the point where Asia meets the South Pacific. Papua New Guinea is in a stable region of peace and does not anticipate any outside aggression.

The Commander of the Defence Force, Brigadier General E. R. Diro, addresses a parade.

His Royal Highness The Prince Charles inspects a Guard of Honour on his arrival at Jacksons Airport for the Independence celebrations in September, 1975.

The Government places a high priority on developing close ties with its Pacific neighbours, and does not intend to enter into military pacts or alliances with the major world powers. It maintains a Universalist foreign policy and refrains from being critical of ideologies and activities of the great powers.

One of the main functions of the Defence Force is to assist civil authority to maintain law and order in times of national emergency. This situation has not arisen and the Royal Papua New Guinea Constabulary does not require any assistance.

Internal matters wherein the Defence Force has been effective are civil disaster relief and surveillance of the 200-mile Exclusive Economic Zone (EEZ). The fitting of radar and sophisticated navigation equipment to Defence Force aircraft has greatly increased the Force's search and surveillance capability.

The presence of anti-government rebels in the Indonesian province of Irian Jaya is an internal problem for Indonesia. However, the Papua New Guinea Government is aware of the potential dangers in such a situation. In June 1978, Defence Force troops were deployed near the border to prevent rebel elements from crossing the border into Papua New Guinea from Indonesia.

Organisation

The Defence Force is subject to the control of the National Executive Council through the Minister for Defence. There is no office of Commander-in-Chief, and all orders and instructions to the Defence Force must be given by or through the Commander.

There is a Defence Council comprising the Minister for Defence, the Secretary of the Department of Defence, and the Commander of the Defence Force. The Defence Council supervises the administration of the Defence Force and the Department, determines the terms and conditions of Defence Force members, and issues Council orders.

The Defence organisation is composed of five branches. Two branches — Policy and Planning, Finance and Programming — are primarily civilian and report directly to the Secretary. The others — Operations, Personnel and Logistics — are military and are directly under the Commander.

Land Element

The land element consists of two infantry battalions of the Pacific Islands Regiment (PIR), an engineer battalion, and various support units.

The First Battalion (1PIR) is based at Taurama Barracks near Port Moresby while the Second Battalion (2PIR) is based at Moem Barracks in Wewak, East Sepik Province. The Engineer Battalion has its headquarters at Murray Barracks, and has companies based there and at Taurama Barracks.

The support organisations include signals, transport, supply, workshop and military police. They have their headquarters in Port Moresby and have units or detachments at the various Defence Force barracks throughout the country.

The main activity of the PIR is a programme of patrolling which covers all parts of the country. The objectives of these patrols are to exercise the troops in their operational role, to gain and maintain the goodwill of the people, and to collect topographical information. While on patrol, soldiers sometimes carry out minor civic action tasks in consultation with local officials. They help build water tank stands, bridges and sports facilities, and help repair school buildings and aid posts.

Training exercises are conducted regularly to test and maintain the operational readiness of the Defence Force. In July 1979, the Force conducted a 14-day exercise code-named "Kumul One" at Gurney in the Milne Bay Province. The exercise involved about 1 000 servicemen from Papua New Guinea and Australia.

Each battalion of the PIR and the engineer battalion likewise conduct smaller scale exercises in infantry tactics and internal security duties in the training areas near their bases. Each infantry company in turn goes through "sub-unit" training, which includes patrolling, ambushing, raids, etc.

The majority of civic action tasks are carried out by the engineer battalion and the preventive medicine platoon. The biggest task undertaken by the engineer battalion so far is the West Sepik project which was completed in September 1977. The project involved the building of a new all-weather airfield, a hard landing for rivercraft, and a network of roads at the Green River outstation, near the border with Irian Jaya. The battalion's major task last year was the construction of a road in New Ireland linking the agricultural areas of the Lelet Plateau with markets on the east coast.

The main activities of the preventive medicine platoon last year were two immunisation tasks in the Simbu Province and an anthropological survey in Madang Province. Doctors and dentists with the platoon also extend their services to the civilian population particularly where medical services are limited, such as at Lombrum in the Manus Province.

A popular unit of the Defence Force is the Pipes and Drums of the two Pacific Islands Regiment battalions. These band platoons are in constant demand for provincial celebrations and have participated in several major Australian city celebrations. Recently the Pipes and Drums played in the Solomon Islands independence celebrations held on 7 July 1978.

The Pipes and Drums bands of the two Pacific Islands Regiment battalions perform at official parades and many public functions.

The PNGDF Engineer Batalion on a road building action project.

A Soldier of the Defence Force Land Element practice grenade throwing.

Maritime Element

The maritime element consists of the patrol boat squadron of five attack class patrol boats and the landing craft squadron of two landing craft.

The patrol boat squadron is based at Lombrum Naval Base, Manus Province. It is responsible for patrolling the territorial waters of Papua New Guinea, visiting coastwatchers and remote areas, and collecting information and intelligence. The squadron's role of fisheries surveillance has gained further importance with the declaration of the 200-mile Exclusive Economic Zone for Papua New Guinea in April 1978. Patrol boats have arrested a number of foreign fishing vessels straying into the declared zone and have warned off several more.

Other important activities of the squadron include search and rescue operations, medical evacuation of villagers in remote places, and reporting on non-functioning navigational aids and other dangers to navigation.

The primary purpose of the landing craft squadron is to provide logistic support to other elements of the Defence Force. The squadron is always fully occupied providing this support, its two ships doing periodic freight runs from Port Moresby to northern Defence Force bases, carrying equipment and bulk stores not suitable for air transport.

Gunnery practice on a PNGDF Sea Element patrol boat.

The squadron plays a large part in the engineer battalion's operations where it is required to deploy and extract heavy engineer plant and equipment. It also helps ship various freight for government departments and communities, ranging from electric generators to tons of rocks for civic action projects.

A small team of divers from the explosive disposal unit, get rid of World War II explosives and bombs in the country. The divers are often utilised by provincial authorities in civic action tasks such as blasting channels through reefs, search and rescue, minor salvage and underwater surveys.

Air Element

The air element, the newest and smallest arm of the Defence Force, is based in Lae, Morobe Province. It comprises the Air Transport Squadron (ATS) equipped with four DC 3 and three Nomad aircraft.

The ATS provides air support to Defence Force establishments and units. This involves resupplying patrols by air and transporting troops and civilians. The other functions of the ATS are search and rescue, civic action and squadron training.

With the proclaiming of the 200-mile zone, the three Nomads have been refitted with radar, VLF Omega navigation equipment and long-range fuel tanks. This has enabled the aircraft to effectively patrol the entire declared area and in conjunction with the patrol boats, discourage the intrusion of unlicensed fishing vessels.

Training

The Defence Force has three major training institutions — the PNGDF Trade Training Depot, the PNGDF Trade Training Unit and the PNG Joint Services College.

Initial training of members of the Defence Force is carried out at the Training Depot located at the Goldie River Barracks outside Port Moresby. Some trade and officer promotion training is also conducted at the depot.

Apprentices who pass initial training at the depot undergo a two-year intensive apprentice training at the Trade Training Unit at Murray Barracks. The final two years are spent gaining practical experience alongside qualified tradesmen at the General Engineering Workshop or any of the Defence Force establishments. In the case of aircraft tradesmen, they have to pass the gruelling CAA examinations for aircraft crew.

Selected soldiers are trained to become officers at the Joint Services College at Igam Barracks in Lae, Morobe Province. Officers from the other disciplined forces in Papua New Guinea (Police and Corrective Institutions) are also trained at the college.

Considerable time is spent on citizenship training and in educating selected soldiers in both military and civil occupations. The Defence Force sponsors students at the University of Papua New Guinea, the PNG University of Technology and in other tertiary institutions.

Defence Co-operation

In recent years Papua New Guinea has continued to increase its defence contacts with other countries, particularly those in the South Pacific region.

Notable instances of such co-operation were the training of officer cadets from the Gilbert Islands (now Kiribati) and the Joint Services College in 1977 and the participation of the Pipes and Drums Band of the PNG Defence Force in the independence celebrations of the Solomon Islands.

The Government has approved the seeking of defence aid from New Zealand and negotiations are underway to draw up a Visiting Forces Agreement and Defence Co-operation Programme between Papua New Guinea and New Zealand.

The major part of foreign defence assistance received by Papua New Guinea comes from Australia. Papua New Guinea maintains a Defence Co-operation Programme with Australia under which the latter continues to provide the services of loan personnel to the PNG Defence Force. Australia still maintains about 220 officers, mainly in technical and specialised positions, in the PNG Defence Force.

Under the Defence Co-operation Programme, Australia pays for salaries of Australian loan personnel in Papua New Guinea, the costs of training PNG Defence Force personnel in Australia, and costs associated with agreed defence projects as well as Australian units operating in Papua New Guinea.

The Australian Government spends more than $A14 million every year for this programme.

Tourism:

Papua New Guinea — with its varied scenery, interesting history, rich culture, friendly people, political stability and sound economy, among other factors — has a lot of attractions to offer visitors.

The country has had casual visitors for almost a century but only in recent years has it become interested in organised tourism. Facilities for visitors are being increased and improved, including transport and accommodation.

A large proportion of demand for accommodation comes from people visiting on business or for professional reasons. Existing hotels in Papua New Guinea compare favourably with those in major cities in other countries. Furthermore, most towns in Papua New Guinea have inexpensive guest houses and hostels that provide good accommodation.

Attractions

The tourist attractions of Papua New Guinea are almost as varied as the number of regions and provinces in the country.

The Southern Region (composed of the National Capital District, Central Province, Milne Bay Province, Gulf Province and Western Province) offers attractions different from those of the Northern Region (Northern and Morobe Provinces).

In addition, the attractions of the New Guinea Islands Region (comprising New Ireland, Manus, East New Britain, West New Britain, Madang, North Solomons, East Sepik and West Sepik) are relatively distinct from those of the Highlands Region (Eastern Highlands, Western Highlands, Southern Highlands, Enga and Chimbu).

International traffic counter, Jacksons Airport.

National Capital District. In many ways, this is the most important area in the country. It is the seat of the National Government (located mainly at Waigani), the official residence of the Governor-General, the National Parliament and the headquarters of all Government departments.

The national airline (Air Niugini) and many of the country's biggest commercial and industrial companies have their head offices in this District. The embassies and consular offices of countries having diplomatic ties with Papua New Guinea are also located here.

Places of interest include Ela Beach, St. Mary's Cathedral (built in Sepik "Haus Tambaran" style), Hanuabada village, the National Museum and Art Gallery, the modern campus of the University of Papua New Guinea, and the world-famous orchid collection in the National Botanic Gardens. Loloata Island Resort provides walks, snorkelling, shell hunting and fishing.

A hall at the National Museum and Art Gallery, Waigani.

Port Moresby, the main centre of the National Capital District, is the capital city of Papua New Guinea. The City, with its large international airport (Jacksons) and busy harbour (Fairfax), is the main gateway to the country. It is named after Sir Fairfax, father of Captain John Moresby, who explored the area.

The Port Moresby Show, held in June every year, consists of cultural, agricultural and industrial presentations. Another yearly cultural event is the Hiri Moale Festival which is held in September.

Modern accommodation and entertainment facilities are available at the city's Gateway Hotel, Travelodge Hotel, Papua Hotel, Hotel Moresby, Davara Motel, Islander Hotel, Sunam Outrigger Model and Boroko Hotel. The Civic Guest House, Salvation Army Hostel and Young Women's Christian Association provide low-priced accommodation.

There are also several good restaurants, cinema houses and duty-free stores in the city.

Several travel agencies in Port Moresby arrange travel not only in the National Capital District but also throughout the country.

Traditional dancers at the Port Moresby Show.

A dining room of the Islander Hotel, Port Moresby.

Central Province. The late film star, Errol Flynn, settled on the banks of the Laloki River in the Province and fell in love with a local girl. He had a plantation but it was not successful.

There is a scenic drive up the Sogeri Valley to the Varirata National Park which features two walking tracks through bushland inhabited

A crocodile at the Moitake wildlife sanctuary.

for hundreds of years by tree-dwelling Koiari people.

Hombrum's Bluff Lookout is a good vantage point to view the surrounding countryside and the Coral Sea. Other tourist attractions in the area are the Rouna Falls, the Sogeri rubber plantations, and McDonald's and Ower's Corner at the beginning of the Kokoda Trail, scenes of bitter fighting in World War II. Accommodation facilities in the area include the Rouna and Kokoda Trail Motel.

Another historical landmark is the Bomana War Cemetery where about 4 000 servicemen, killed in the Pacific War, are buried. Close to the cemetery is the Moitake wildlife sanctuary which includes a crocodile farm.

To the east, Marshall Lagoon, with its quiet harbour and nearby Cape Rodney settlement scheme, provide additional attractions for holiday makers and sightseers. Also of interest is Tapini to the west which is excellent for bush walking or mountain climbing. Accommodation is available at the Tapini Hotel.

The Central Province is noted for its Mekeo dancers and an artifact centre, Village Arts, which stocks over 20 000 artifacts from different areas of the country.

Other tourist areas are Woitape and Yule Island which have the Oro Guest House and Rabao Mareana Hotel for visitors respectively.

A village in the highlands of the Central Province.

Milne Bay Province. The Province takes its name from the deeply-indented Milne Bay. It is basically a marine province consisting of about 1 000 islands, islets and atolls.

Tourist development is concentrated on the Trobriand Islands whose main attractions are the traditional houses, dresses and dances of the islanders and the distinctive artifacts offered for sale at reasonable prices.

The most popular part of the Trobriand Group is Kiriwina Island. Speedboats are available for hire from Kiriwina Lodge which can provide operators. The Kiriwina islanders celebrate a three-month (June-August) Yam Festival during which they hold traditional dancing and music, and make of ceremonial gift exchanges to mark the yam harvest.

Another interesting place is Samarai which is noted for its Pearl Festival. It is a two-day event in November which features handcraft displays, canoe racing, sporting events and a beauty contest.

Good accommodation is available at the Samarai Guest House and also at the Masurina Lodge in Alotau, the provincial capital.

Mekeo dancer at Bereina, Central Province.
Dancers from the Marshall Lagoon area, Central Province.

Rusa deer at the Bensbach Wildlife Lodge.

Gulf and Western Provinces. These two provinces cover the whole of the western part of what was formerly Papua, right up to the Indonesian border. They contain the big rivers of the Southern mainland: Fly, Strickland, Kikori, Purari and others.

For those who like flying and seeing huge areas of swamps, mangroves, rain forest, river delta and giant streams, the air trip to these Provinces is worthwhile.

The Gulf Province has been the scene of intensive oil prospecting since the end of the war. Furthermore, it could be developed for considerable hydro-electricity generating potential in the future.

Accommodation facilities in the Gulf Province include those of Hotel Kerema in the capital, Gulf Hotel at Kikori, and Ihu Guest House at the Ihu Subdistrict.

The main attraction of the Western Province is the Bensbach Wildlife Lodge, particularly for camera enthusiasts. The Bensbach River offers rich fishing (barramundi, black bass, tarpon and saratoga) and abounds with crocodiles. Photographers' delight includes the plains and forests with herds of Rusa deer; and dozens of bird varieties such as the Bensbach Rifle Bird, Birds of Paradise, and cassowaries.

The Daru Hotel and Daru Guest House, in the capital of the Western Province, provide accommodation for visitors.

Northern Province. Much of the coastline offers fine white-sand beaches and in the Cape Nelson area, fingerlike land forms create interesting fiords, bays and covers.

The heart of the fiord country is Tufi, on the tip of Cape Nelson. Tufi's Kofure Village Guest House can be reached by canoe from the airstrip, while Mirigina Lodge is adjacent to the strip on a hill overlooking the Bay.

Further south is Wanigela, noted for its clay pottery and *tapa* cloth. *Tapa* is the name given all over the Pacific for cloth which is made by beating the bark of a tree — the Paper Mulberry, *Brousconetia Papyrisera*. In eastern Papua New Guinea, on the coasts and in the mountains, the women wear *tapa* as wrap-around skirts. The men have it woven between their legs and forming a belt, with one end becoming a short apron in front and the other a long tail hanging down behind. Wallets and bags are also made out of *tapa*.

Wanigela has a plantation resort called Waijuga Park, which is another tourist attraction of the Northern Province.

Kokoda Trail, wartime famous track, is a favourite hiking spot for the fit and adventurous. From Kokoda the road descends through the foothills to Popondetta, the provincial capital. Popondetta provides accommodation at the Lamington Hotel and Popondetta Guest House.

Bringing home the catch, Barramundi fishing near Daru.

A tree kangaroo at Bensbach.

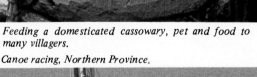

Feeding a domesticated cassowary, pet and food to many villagers.

Deer and wild fowl at Bensbach.

Canoe racing, Northern Province.

Tapa cloth display, Northern Province.

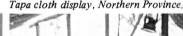

The City of Lae, capital of the Morobe Province is a fast developing centre of population. At the coastal end of the Highlands Highway it is ideally located for many secondary industries. It is a crossroad for tourists travelling to the northern part of the country and the islands.

A safe distance away is Mount Lamington which has a walking track and a campsite in the ridge line.

Morobe Province. It is the country's largest in population: about 300 000. Much of the pre-war wealth of New Guinea came from Morobe in the form of gold. Gold was discovered in the Wau area in 1913. Gold is still obtained but is only a minor industry at present.

The capital city, Lae, is the industrial and commercial centre of Papua New Guinea. Industries based in Lae cover construction of roads, bridges and buildings; packaging; timber processing; oil and petrol; retail and wholesale trading; manufacture of soft drinks, paint, gas, tyres and glass; and engineering, steel fabrication, bakery, laundry dry cleaning, concrete products, printing, rice terminal, wire products and a foundry.

The Lae port handles more inward and outward cargoes than any other port in the country.

The Morobe Show, held at Lae in October every year, displays the commercial, agricultural and cultural development of the Province.

Notable institutions at Lae include the University of Technology, National Posts and Telecommunications Training Centre, and Forest Industry Training Centre. Igam Barracks,

also at Lae, is a military reserve of the Department of Defence and site of the Joint Services College (which trains officers for the Defence Force, Constabulary, Corrective Institutions Service and other agencies).

Among the additional attractions in Lae are the Botanical Gardens, War Memorial and Cemetery, Lae Golf Course, Wagan or Malahang Beach, and Mount Lunaman.

Other landmarks of Morobe include the Nadzab Airport, the Forestry College at Bulolo, and the Wau Ecology Institute, which is dedicated to education and research into tropical living organisms and conservation of the country's plants and animals.

There are several accommodation facilities: Melanesian Hotel, Hotel Cecil, Huon Gulf Motel, Klinkii Lodge, Lae Lodge and the Salvation Army Motel at Lae; Pine Lodge at Bulolo; Dregerhafen Lodge and Finschhafen Community Hostel at Finschaffen; and Paradise Springs Resort at Sialum. Besides Wau Hotel, the Wau Ecology Insitute also provides accommodation.

There are also some good restaurants and cinema houses in the Province. Transport facilities include cars for hire and buses.

The Morobe Province Tourist Association, together with the Government and other

A woman from the Western Highlands in traditional dress.

169

Many World War 2 wrecks still litter old batlefields in Papua New Guinea. A tank and field gun lie where they were put out of action at Siwai in the North Solomons Province (Bougainville Island).

organisations, is helping promote the tourist industry of the Province.

New Ireland Province. It is mainly an old established plantation area whose major crops are copra and cocoa.

The Province has pleasant tropical and coastal scenery, and an excellent road down the east coast. Among the tourist attractions are the reefs, long sandy beaches, beautiful islands and sport fishing. There are remains of the Japanese occupation such as artillery pieces, sunken boats, aircraft, tanks and bunkers.

Kavieng, the capital, is a pretty little town with a good airport. The National Fisheries College, located at Kavieng, has been a big boost to the fishing industry in New Ireland in particular and the country in general.

Aside from Kavieng Hotel, visitors are welcome at the Malangan Guest House.

Manus Province. Although it is the smallest province, Manus occupies an important position in the country's history. During the war, the Japanese occupied Manus beginning in April 1942. The Japanese occupation lasted until February 1944 when American and Australian

Broken aircraft, like this wartime transport plane at Hayfield in the East Sepik Province, stand as a memorial to those who fought and died in Papua New Guinea during World War 2. Many are protected by the government as war relies.

troops landed at Momote and recaptured the Province for the Allies.

The Americans developed the Province's Seeadler Harbour into a first-class naval base and upgraded Momote airstrip to take in heavy bombers. In a few months Manus Island became one of the biggest naval bases in the Pacific, with hundreds of ships in its harbour and nearly a million troops on its shores. It became a jump-off point for the Allied invasion of the Philippines.

Shortly after it was developed, Manus was deserted. Only the wharves, warehouses and shore establishments remained. But such development had a considerable impact on the local people who witnessed what white people could do and now wanted to have part of the knowledge that had brought such things about. In the following years, the people were educated in a comparatively short time. Real economic progress, however, followed gradually.

Lorengau, the capital, has accommodation available at the Lorengau Hotel and Seeadler Lodge. The Defence Force has a naval base at Lombrum near Lorengau.

East New Britain Province. It is known for its scenic beauty and rich war history. From the volcanic activity at Rabaul, the capital, is derived the Province's main attributes: the picturesque Simpson Harbour around which Rabaul is built, and the rich volcanic soil.

Throughout the Province are remnants of the German era and Japanese occupation. At Kokopo is the grave of the legendary Queen Emma of Samoa, who established plantations in the Duke of York Island in the 1870s.

Namanula Hill features vast orchid gardens and the remains of the first German residency. War relics are found at the Coastwatchers Memorial Lookout where a Japanese Zero and anti-artillery guns are situated.

Along Kokopo road are deep tunnels set into volcanic walls in which Japanese forces stored their barges. At Bitapaka is a war cemetery where Papua New Guinean, Australian, Chinese and Indian soldiers, who died during the war in the Rabaul area, are buried.

'Frangipani Queen' and 'Mr East New Britain'.

Japanese barge in a tunnel off the Kokopo road.

Two big cultural events are celebrated each year in the Province. The Frangipani Festival, staged in July to commemorate the annual blooming of the Frangipani flower, features the selections of a Frangipani Queen and a "Mr East New Britain", a float parade, mardi gras, and sports events. The Tolai Warwargira Festival, held later in the year, is highlighted by a weekend of string bands, traditional music and choral singing.

Rabaul is the headquarters for a plantation management training programme administered by the Department of Commerce. The programme aims to assist in the development and localisation of plantation managers by training talented staff to operate plantations effectively.

Rabaul has seven accommodation houses, namely: Rabaul Travelodge, Hotel Ascot, Kulau Lodge, Luaina Lodge, Orim's Lodge, Motel Kaivuna and Rabaul Community Hostel. Cars are available for hire.

The New Britain Tourist Association, together with the Government and other organisations, is helping promote the tourist industry of the Province.

West New Britain Province. Considerable potential exists in the Province for tourism. Hot springs, wild fowl egg grounds, active volcanoes, tropical beaches, and pleasant swimming and fishing conditions could all provide attractions for tourists.

The nucleus for tourist development is the area around Kimbe (the capital), Hoskins, and Talasea. The area has a good road network and accommodation facilities in (Palm Lodge Motel and Hoskins Hotel).

Oil palm is the success story of West New Britain. The industry is centred around two areas: Hoskins-Kimbe and Bialla. The Hoskins oil palm project has been producing about 150 500 tonnes of fresh fruit bunches with an annual export value of about K10.5 million. Estate plantings cover 2 735 hectares; village plantings, 642 hectares; and resettlement plantings, 5 700 hectares.

Madang Province. Tourism is one of Madang's main industries. The Madang Tourist Association has been actively promoting Madang's natural beauty and numerous scenic spots. For example, the Association has been promoting the Maborasa Festival, a yearly exhibition of *singsing*, demonstrations of carvings, artifacts, and other cultural shows.

'*Traditional' carvings for the tourist trade.*

Distinctive clay pots and dishes from the Murik Lakes area of the Sepik river.

Spirit figures protect the entrance to a council house.

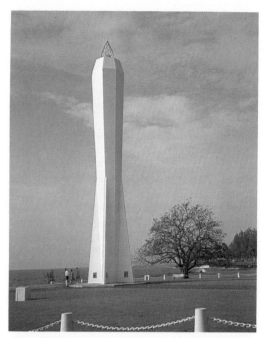

The Coastwatcher's Memorial and lighthouse at Madang.

Madang has a lot of other tourist attractions. Approached from the sea, the first landmark at Madang is a 30-metre high memorial to fallen wartime coastwatchers, the Coastwatchers Lighthouse. Madang town likewise has its old German cemetery, Chinatown, market and artifact shops, and orchid gardens.

"Anyone for golf?" at the Madang Golf course.

For the sportsman, Madang offers a fine golf course, and several squash and tennis courts. Scuba diving around the coral reefs and the many wartime wrecks is popular. Facilities for sailing, water-skiing and game fishing are available.

Out of town are Yabob and Bilibil villages with their traditional pottery; and Siar village with its colourful houses and *singsings*.

Madang has pleasant hotels, including Hotel Madang Resort and Plantation Hotel. The other accommodation houses are the Coast-watchers Motel, Smugglers Inn, and Country Women's Association (CWA) Cottage.

The large industries in Madang are the Jant and Wewak Timbers which form the biggest timber industry of its kind in Papua New Guinea. Madang Slipways provides shipwright and engineering services for many coastal vessels plying Papua New Guinea waters. It services an average of 40 ships of up to 500 tonnes weight every year.

North Solomons Province. Formerly called Bougainville (which name is retained by the main island in the Province), North Solomons is world famous for its enormous open-cut copper mine at Panguna. The mine, which also produces silver and gold, is the most important development to the Province and one of the major foreign exchange earning industries of Papua New Guinea.

Points of interest include Mount Bagana, Lake Luloru, Lake Mitchell and plantations along the coastline. Charter flights to these places can be arranged with Bougair, a third-level airline based in the provincial capital, Arawa.

Bougair also operates services to Buka, Boku, Buin, Kieta and other locations in the Province. Buka is noted for its basketware.

Beautiful baskets are woven in many parts of the country.

Arora Island, just off Kieta, offers pleasant picnic, swimming and diving among white sands and clear water tropical reefs.

Accommodation is available at Buka (Buka Luman Soho Guest House) and Kieta (Davara Motel and Hotel Kieta). There are cars for hire at Kieta.

East Sepik Province. The Province is considered as the home of some of the riches forms of Papua New Guinea art and culture. Its people are among the best artists of the country. The products of their creativity are acknowledged as the finest examples of primtive art in the world.

Located in the Province is the Sepik River — the largest in Papua New Guinea. The River is one of the most remarkable reservoirs of crocodiles, butterflies, birds and orchids. Huge "Haus Tambarans" or spirit houses soar up to a hundred feet, dominating the villages which line the River and some of the roads to the interior.

Local businessmen and groups are increasingly taking part in the tourist industry. Hire canoes in Wewak (the capital), tour bus charters, taxi service and artifact sales are part of the participation in tourism by the local people.

Through charter aircraft, tour buses and speedboats, the remotest reaches of the Sepik area can be visited in relative comfort. A luxurious way to visit the area is to board a houseboat, which runs a three-day shuttle between Pagwi and Angoram.

Houseboat on the Sepik River.

Accommodation facilities include the Wewa Wewak Hotel, Angoram Hotel, Maprik Waken Hotel, Sepik Motel, Windjammer Beach Motel and Karawari Lodge which offer exceptional tours by river truck to remote villages where ancient cultural practices are re-enacted.

West Sepik Province. The provincial capital, Vanimo, is located on a peninsula outlined by a magnificent white sand beach. From Vanimo, visitors can drive within reach of the border between Papua New Guinea and the Irian Jaya Province of Indonesia.

Telefomin, an inland patrol post accessible from Vamino, is a remote valley known for its scenery, caves and beautiful artifacts.

Aitape, on the north coast, is known for an abundance of war relics, particularly at Tadji Airfield, a wartime airstrip. Aitape is also noted for its fine beaches, lush vegetation and nearby coral islands.

Narimo Hotel in Vanimo provides accommodation and a bus or car tour to the Indonesian border.

Peaceful beach scene near Vanimo.

The Vanimo airstrip.

Eastern Highlands Province. The Province has been drawing tourists for years with its cultural displays and other attractions. Its Asaro mudmen and the Raun Raun Travelling Theatre, through their successful performances locally and overseas, have been bringing fame for Eastern Highlands and Papua New Guinea.

The Eastern Highlands Show, held every two years in Goroka (the provincial capital), combines *singsings* with an agricultural exhibition. The next show is scheduled to be held in 1980.

Asaro mudmen take a rest at the Goroka Show.

A traditional funeral in the highlands calls for a coat of mud on the mourners.

The J.K. McCarthy Museum at Goroka and handcraft shops in the Province are a worthy showcase of the people's rich culture.

There are a number of hotels and guest houses for visitors, namely, the Bird of Paradise Hotel, Lantern Lodge, Minogere Lodge, and CWA Cottage in Goroka; Kainantu Lodge in Kainantu; and Salvation Army Flats in both Goroka and Kainantu.

The Travel Association of Papua New Guinea and Trans Niugini Tours are both based in Goroka. The latter promotes travel to the

175

A fearsome line up of charcoal blackened dancers from the Western Highlands Province.

Two elderly participants at a highlands show carr, the traditional ceremonial stone axe.

Eastern Highlands as well as the Sepik and Western Provinces. Transport facilities at Goroka include cars and buses for hire.

The K30 million Ramu hydro-electric scheme – the largest in the country – is located at Yonki in the Province and supplies power to central mainland centres.

Goroka is the headquarters of the National Institute of Medical Research; and Talair, the country's biggest third-level airline.

Western Highlands Province. The Province is noted for its colourful *singsings,* particularly during the Mount Hagen Show which is held every two years.

Another major tourist attraction is the Baiyer River Bird Sanctuary which features about 90 species of birds and animals of Papua New Guinea. It is within easy reach (55 kilometres north of Mount Hagen, the capital) and has a lodge for visitors.

Other accommodation facilities in the Province include the Airport Hotel, Highlander Hotel, Banz Hotel, Hagen Park Motel, Minj Hotel and Kimininga Hostel. Cars for hire and buses are available. In addition, tours can be arranged.

There are sports organisations, namely: Mount Hagen Bowling Club, Mount Hagen Golf Club, and Wahgi Valley Sports Club.

Parrots and a white cockatoo at the wildlife sanctuary at Baiyer River.

Southern Highlands Province. Its singular distinction among the Highlands Provinces is that its first base camp, set up in 1937 on Lake Kutubu, was established and serviced by seaplane. Catalina aircraft were used to service the outposts. Patrols from this headquarters contacted most of the people in the eastern half of the Province.

Southern Highlanders are a colourful people. Each area of the Province boasts its own distinctive ornamentation. The Taris have their brilliant wigs made of human hair and yellow everlasting daisies. The Ialibus have Bird of Paradise plumes and woven red helmets, while the Mendis and Nipas have cassowary plumes.

The Atea Kanada in the Southern Highlands is considered as one of the most spectacular river-cave systems in the world. Local and foreign cave scientists have explored the system extensively.

Hospitality awaits visitors at Hotel Mendi in the provincial capital.

Colourful wigmen of the Tari basin display finery at the market.

Keglsugl airstrip, the country's highest, lies in the shadow of the highest mountain, Mt Wilhelm, which stands sentinel at the junction of the Chimbu, Madang and Eastern Highlands Provinces.

Enga Province. Formerly a part of the Western and Southern Highlands Provinces, Enga became a province in 1973. "Enga" is a Melpa term for "the people to the West".

Many of the people still dress traditionally. Men wear aprons and tufts of leaves, and normally carry axes. Women wear dried-grass drapes and pandanus-leaf capes, and carry net bags.

Engas practise some interesting customs, one of which is the Tee Festival. This is their traditional way of showing appreciation for personal favours received from relatives and friends by exchanging pigs, pearl shells and ceremonial axes. The ceremony, held publicly, includes a parade with pigs and cassowaries, and *singsings*.

Tourist spots include the Enga Cultural Centre at Wabag (the capital); and Lake Iviva, in the Lagaip District, which offers good sailing, water skiing and carp fishing. Others are the Yampu Weaving Centre, Yogos and Pompabus sheep projects, the Laiagam orchid garden, and traditional salt-producing pools.

Club facilities exist at the Wabag and Lagaip Country Clubs. Wabag Lodge, operated by Talair, provides accommodation.

Chimbu Province. Mount Wilhelm — the country's highest mountain (4 509 metres) — has its peak in the north of the Province, which is also called Simbu.

The tourist spots of the Province include other spectacular mountain and gorge scenery in the Highlands, namely, Mount Elimbari and the Chimbu gorge, both with extensive cave formations. The Wahgi and Marigl valleys, accessible by road, also attract tourists.

Some of Papua New Guinea's most spectacularly-located airfields are in the Province. The Kundiawa Airport, in the provincial capital, has been described as the "nearest approach to an aircraft carrier on dry land". The Keglsugl Aerodrome, at 2 720 metres, is the country's highest airfield.

The people of the Province usually refer to themselves as Chimbu only when in other parts of the country or when addressing visitors from elsewhere. Otherwise they identify themselves by reference to their clan, tribe or locality. They seldom eat meat except during traditional ceremonies and festivals.

The Province offers visitors two accommodation choices: Kundiawa Hotel or Chimbu Lodge.

Promotion

The Office of Tourism, under the Ministry of Commerce, Industry and Tourism, is responsible for the control, direction and promotion of tourism.

The role of the Office of Tourism includes acting as a channel for the viewpoints of the private sector and for communicating their needs to the Government. This is achieved through the Tourism Advisory Council (representing the private sector) and the Tourism Co-ordinating Committee (representing the Government).

The Office of Tourism works closely with Air Niugini in joint production of promotional material, in overseas promotions, seminars and exhibitions; and in joint attendance at international travel conferences. It has appointed public relations/marketing-travel consultants in Japan, the United Kingdom and Europe.

The Tourism Office represents Papua New Guinea as an active Government member of the Pacific Area Travel Association (PATA), which is based in San Francisco in the United States. It arranged for the formation of a PATA Area Chapter for Papua New Guinea which consists of officials of travel and tourist organisation in the country.

The Office of Tourism has won top prizes in three PATA competitions. In 1978, the film "Sounds Like Niugini" won the Best Film Award. In 1979, the country's National Theatre Company was highly acclaimed for its cultural performance, and Papua New Guinea was also awarded first prize in the tourism poster contest.

The Office of Tourism is likewise a member of the Pacific Islands Tourism Development Council, which seeks to promote tourism to Pacific island-member nations.

Development wise, the Office of Tourism is actively pursuing policies of providing new, and building up existing attractions, suitable not only for tourists but of importance and interest to residents. The latest projects include an Oceanarium and Theme Park for Ela Beach in Port Moresby and a 300-room international-style hotel for the National Capital District.

A sport fishing project is under investigation in the Northern and Milne Bay Provinces. Other areas are also being studied for suitable tourist involvement.

Advice to tourists

When in Papua New Guinea, tourists are advised to observe the following general "Do's and Dont's":

- Don't tip. To give service to the stranger is an honour in our Melanesian culture. Nor do we add a service charge to your hotel or restaurant bill.
- Do be friendly. A smile and a wave (our children almost demand it), or a halting phrase in Pidgin, especially when you are travelling through the countryside, will win you many friends.
- Don't be afraid to bargain when you are buying artifacts in the villages.
- Do drive carefully, especially in the country. If you are unlucky enough to hit a wandering chicken or pig, grin and pay up. If you have an accident and someone is hurt, take yourself straight off to the nearest police station and report it.
- Don't always expect a smooth ride. In our developing country, ten miles of all-weather road are more valuable than one of multi-lane motorway.
- Do dress comfortably but appropriately. Bikinis or supertight shorts are frowned on away from the beach or pool. So are too-open signs of affection.
- Don't ask for trouble by wandering alone at night. Every society has its rascals.
- Do check first if you want to walk off the beaten track or camp. Ask the nearest Provincial Government Office for advice and permission. And don't pick fruit — it belongs to someone.
- Don't expect everything to happen on the dot. The pace of tropical life is often leisurely, but "Melanesian Time" is usually much sooner than *manana* (tomorrow).

For a more enjoyable and rewarding stay in Papua New Guinea, tourists are urged to take note of the following particular pointers:

Clothing. Dress is light, casual and informal. "Tropical formal" evening dress implies a safari suit or open-neck shirt with light slacks.

For ladies, loose dresses, short or long, are probably more comfortable than slacks. Either can be appropriate in the evening. Look for the good local designs incorporating Papua New Guinean prints.

Cotton or cotton/synthetic materials,

preferably drip-dry, are ideal. But avoid 100 per cent synthetic materials which can become sticky in the often-humid climate.

In the Highlands Region, the days are warm but the nights can be chilly. 25°C falling to 14°C (77°F to 57°F), sometimes with a light night frost. Light woollen slacks and shirts, with a handy sweater, are advised unless you come from a very cool climate.

Footwear. Women should be careful to take comfortable well broken-in shoes. Stockings are not usually worn.

Tight shoes on bare feet in conditions of heat and humidity can quickly result in blisters. Open sandals, although cool, have obvious disadvantages under bush conditions or where the roads are rough and without footpaths.

Headgear. Don't expose yourself to the risk of sunstroke. Remember to wear a hat — even in the Highlands. A wide-brimmed hat will protect your face from the vertical sun around noon.

Health. If coming from or through endemic-cholera or yellow-fever areas, you will need to show a certificate of vaccination against these diseases.

In Papua New Guinea, the malaria-bearing mosquito is still found in certain parts of the country despite a vigorous eradication campaign. It is recommended that, for not less than two weeks before arrival, during your whole visit, and for four weeks after leaving the country, take a regular dose of the country's approved anti-malarial preparation.

Your doctor can give you a prescription. And while you are in Papua New Guinea, these preparations are available without prescription from pharmacies.

Food. You will be agreeably surprised by the choice and quality of meals available in hotels and restaurants. Vegetables are often locally grown and beautifully fresh, and high-quality beef and poultry from the Highlands and the coast are usually on the menu.

The seas swarm with fish, and particularly good are barramundi, crayfish, prawns and crabs. The fast Highlands streams produce fine trout.

Local fruits should not be missed, including pineapples, papayas, mangoes, passionfruit, bananas, and strawberries.

Breakfast in hotels can be Continental-style or English, with eggs and bacon, toast and marmalade. Lunch is usually served between 12 and 2 pm. Dinner is normally available between 7 and 9 pm.

Drinks. Hotels and restaurants serve Arabica and Robusta coffee as well as high-quality tea. These are produced in the Highlands and have become world famous.

Papua New Guinea is also proud of its local beer produced by two brewery companies. Good Australian and European wines are imported. Soft drinks and mixers are inexpensive.

Money. Foreign currencies may be exchanged into the local currency — kina and toea — at commercial banks and the currency exchange desk at Jacksons Airport.

Exchange your money before leaving Papua New Guinea. You will get less for your kina back home.

Shopping. Papua New Guinea is world famous for the cultural range and variety of craftwork made by its people in wood, copper, pottery, shell or basketwork. You will find artifact shops in every centre and often in your hotel lobby. When you are in the rural areas, you can buy them through the missions or direct from the village craftsmen.

There is, however, a stringent control on the export of artifacts of national, historical or cultural significance. This includes those made before 1960, which incorporate human remains or the feathers of protected birds like the Bird of Paradise. If in doubt, refer to the artifact shop owner or the Curator of Anthropology of the National Museum and Art Gallery in Port Moresby.

Main centres offer a sophisticated range of shops and supermarkets where you can find virtually anything you want. There are many Chinese trade stores offering cane and camphor-wood gifts, furniture and oriental fabrics.

Look out for good local pottery, batik cloth and decorative hangings as well as sculptures, paintings and prints by local artists. See and buy the local cultured pearls (duty free), equal to others in the world, and often mounted by craftsmen into fine settings using local gold.

Photography. In the major centres (Port Moresby, Lae, Rabaul and Madang), you will find adequate stocks of films to suit most cameras. In the small centres, it is wise not to depend too much on them. If your film requirements are unusual, take adequate supplies with you.

You can have films developed and printed in the bigger towns, although the service is not always a "same-day" one. Try to protect your unused films from as much heat and humidity as possible and, once used, get them processed as soon as possible. Don't leave films in your camera longer than necessary as the heat and damp make them stick.

There are some tricks to taking good photographs in the tropics. If you are not sure of your light values, ask a local expert or film supplier.

Cleanliness. Littering is an offence which carries a K100 fine. Everybody is requested to co-operate with the Government in its cleanliness campaign.

Sports. Papua New Guinea is one of the most sports-conscious nations in the world.

You can participate in or watch a large variety of activities. These include swimming, reef diving, water skiing, sailing, mountain climbing and pot-holing, bush-walking, bird-watching, orchid spotting, sea and river fishing, riding, canoeing and *gumi* racing (the *gumi* is a raft made of a truck of tractor inner tube), tennis, lawn bowls, football, handball, polo, cricket and shooting.

Further assistance. For further information and assistance in your travels to Papua New Guinea, please contact the Director, Office of Tourism, P.O. Box 5644, Boroko, Papua New Guinea or your nearest travel agent.

Prospects

The tourist industry of Papua New Guinea faces bright prospects in the coming years. Visitor numbers are expected to rise significantly because of the increasing interest of international airlines, the pioneering of new routes by Air Niugini to such places as the United States and South-East Asia, and the restructuring of Pacific region air fares.

Internal demand for accommodation will also increase significantly. This is because of the high rate of national development forecast and the possible commencement of large projects such as the Ok Tedi Copper Mine. The following table reflects the need for a total of 1 302 extra hotel rooms throughout the country from 1979 to 1985.

HOTEL ROOM PROJECTIONS

Year	Visitors	Rooms Required	Additional Rooms Required Annually
1978	34 866	2 003 $^{(*)}$	
1979	43 391	2 109	106
1980	50 685	2 254	145 (251)
1981	63 731	2 424	170 (421)
1982	82 468	2 660	236 (657)
1983	101 436	2 913	253 (910)
1984	119 695	3 126	213 (1 123)
1985	134 058	3 305	179 (1 302)

Total additional rooms required = 1 302

(*) Actual
SOURCE: OFFICE OF TOURISM

One special occasion that will boost the country's tourist industry will be the Third South Pacific Festival of Arts which will be held in Port Moresby in 1980.

The two-week (29 June to 12 July) Festival will bring together over 1 000 performers from some 27 countries and island groups of the South Pacific. There will be spectacular displays of dancing, singing, music, flowers, traditional sports, cooking, craftsmanship, drama, films, canoes and houses from the whole region.

The Festival expected to draw some 10 000 to 12 000 tourists to Papua New Guinea.

PHOTOGRAPHIC CREDITS

Most of the photographs featured throughout this book have been obtained from the Office of Information photographic files.

The publishers gratefully acknowledge the use of other photographic contributions in this book as listed below.

Page 2	Roy and Margaret Mackay
Page 4	Air Niugini
Page 14	Cassowary, Roy and Margaret Mackay
Page 25	Man seated, Air Niugini
Page 26	Maureen Mackenzie
Page 27	Maureen Mackenzie
Page 28	Maureen Mackenzie
Page 54	Tony Reed
Page 61	Air Niugini
Page 63	Coffee sorting, Maurice Bryan
Page 71	Shark fishing, Malcolm Kirk
Page 79	Maurine Bryan
Page 101	Oil palm, Air Niugini
Page 104	Tony Reed
Page 116	Boeing aircraft, Air Niugini
Page 160	Top two photographs, PNG Defence Force
Page 166	Rusa Deer, Air Niugini
Page 167	Cassowary, Office of Tourism; Tapa cloth, Air Niugini
Page 173	Artifacts and Golf, Air Niugini
Page 174	Houseboat, Air Niugini
Page 175	Mudmen, Office of Tourism